IN THE
INTERSECTION:
PARTNERSHIPS IN THE NEW PLAY SECTOR

BY DIANE RAGSDALE

Copyright © 2012 by Diane Ragsdale.

This work is made freely available under the terms of the Creative Commons Attribution 3.0 Unported License,
http://creativecommons.org/licenses/by/3.0/

We want you to share, copy, distribute, transmit, remix, and adapt this book. Attribute Diane Ragsdale as the orginal author and Center for the Theater Commons /HowlRound.com as the original publisher.

ISBN: 9781939006004
Library of Congress Control Number: 2012946259

Center for the Theater Commons / HowlRound.com
Emerson College, c/o Office of the Arts
120 Boylston Street
Boston, MA 02116
USA

For inquiries, e-mail editor@howlround.com or call +1 617-824-3017

Printed in the United States of America

Book Design: Very, Inc. Minneapolis, MN

CONTENTS

- **1** INTRODUCTION
- **5** EXECUTIVE SUMMARY

- **29** DAY 1
  HISTORICAL VIEWPOINTS:
  Rocco Landesman and Gregory Mosher
- **49** HOW WE GOT HERE:
  Robert Brunstein
- **67** EVOLUTION OF THE INTERSECTION:
  Contracts
- **87** REFLECTION, REFRACTION, RESPONSE:
  Artists Panel

- **111** DAY 2
  ROUNDTABLE DISCUSSION #1:
  Commercial Producers
- **127** ROUNDTABLE DISCUSSION #2:
  Nonprofit Producers
- **149** ROUNDTABLE DISCUSSION #3:
  Artists and Others
- **163** FULL GROUP DISCUSSION
- **195** TOWARDS THE CREATION OF A STATEMENT
- **209** ACKNOWLEDGEMENTS
- **211** PARTICIPANTS

INTRODUCTION

This report is the first formal report released by The Center for the Theater Commons, which we have launched in the Office of the Arts at Emerson College in Boston, with the visionary support of Rob Orchard, Executive Director ArtsEmerson, and Emerson's President, Lee Pelton. As such, it marks a milestone in an inquiry that we have been immersed in together for a decade now: an attempt to understand and advance the infrastructure for new works and the artists who make them in this country. We are grateful to Emerson for making a home for the Commons and to our Commons colleagues, Jamie Gahlon and Vijay Mathew, for their work on this publication.

But, more importantly, it builds on a conversation that some of the participants have been engaged in for thirty years. All of us at The Commons have been moved by, and grateful, for the openness of spirit and mind, in particular, of two of its original voices. Rocco Landesman and Gregory Mosher first wrestled with the question of this intersection in the very public forum of *The New York Times* back in 1988. In the intervening decades both their roles and their opinions on the practice of blending commercial and nonprofit resources have evolved dramatically. If it had not been for their capacity for frank and impassioned assessment of their own changing understanding of this intersection, this discussion would not have taken place. Moreover, their open engagement of their own questions in the presence of their colleagues has now inspired the participants in the gathering documented in this report to an equally open and public examination and led to the release of this carefully documented and detailed report from Diane Ragsdale.

It is important to acknowledge the role of The Andrew W. Mellon Foundation in the planning and preparation for the gathering, in the meeting itself, and in the production of this publication. It is equally important to acknowledge the leadership role of the report's author in the many stages that led to this publication.

The Foundation, for its part, hosted the initial conversation in the Fall of 2010 that sparked the commitment of key participants to support and contribute to the planning of the gathering documented here. Ms. Ragsdale provided the impetus for that first conversation and served as its facilitator. This was where Mr. Mosher and Mr. Landesman first shared with each other the developments in their own thinking in the decades since their debate in the pages of *The Times*. A January 2011 planning meeting at Arena Stage in Washington, DC, was also supported by the Foundation and attended by Ms. Ragsdale, where a broader group of commercial and nonprofit producers laid the groundwork for the convening that this report documents. Ms. Ragsdale is currently researching the evolution in the relationship between the commercial and nonprofit theater over the past three decades, and we are grateful for her participation, her expertise, and her insight.

> Once we made the choice to produce our plays not to recoup an investment but to recoup some corner of the universe for our understanding and enlargement, we entered the same world as the university, the museum, the church and became, like them, an instrument of civilization.—Zelda Fichandler

This quote is pulled from Zelda's testimony in the legislative debate over extending the benefits of nonprofit status to theater companies in the United States. Over the decades that have passed since this stark and persuasive distinction was made between the nation's regional theaters and the commercial sector, the practices, environment, and roles have shifted so completely as to render it quaint, perhaps even obsolete. Many commercial producers claim an equal stake in the pursuit of "our understanding and enlargement" and point to new territory in both form and content that has been opened by their projects. Many nonprofit organizations find themselves producing their plays exactly for the purposes of recouping their investment—in search of earned revenue to balance budgets in a challenging economic and cultural climate, which no longer resembles the world that the pioneers of the regional theater movement set out from.

The practice of commingling the commercial and the nonprofit resources of the American Theater has become an accepted and, it would seem from this gathering, increasingly important one since it debuted with the production of *Big River* in 1984, which is revisited in this report. Both the nonprofit leaders and the commercial producers at the event outline ways in which each sector has become dependent upon the other. But, at the same time, both raise significant doubts and challenges to current standards, priorities, and applications of the practice.

In convening this discussion, and commissioning this report, it has been our hope to open a dialogue around the practice, these doubts, and these challenges as they impact the new works sector that is the focus of The Center for the Theater Commons. As with everything we do here, this is intended as an invitation to participate in an ongoing field-wide inquiry into the state of the infrastructure in this sector.

We framed this discussion as an investigation of an "Intersection" because it seemed to us, as we developed the agenda for the two days of discussion, that this is what it is. Two distinct paths, the commercial path and the nonprofit path, each heading toward its own definitions of success, crossing in these moments of collaboration. How, and whether both parties make it through this intersection and move merrily along their separate paths on the other side seemed to be the central question. As the conversation unfolded, however, the sense of it as an intersection grew murky—are the two paths so distinct anymore? Are the definitions of success so different? Are the roles so clearly defined in the process or practice as to constitute different paths? Is there anything but a head-on collision possible if it is an intersection rather than a merge lane? At one point the central metaphor becomes one of a lifeboat into which all parties have jumped.

You will, we hope, come to your own conclusion on the frame. But we also hope you will find, in this document and in the generosity of the participants in sharing their concerns, values, and discoveries, a path to revisiting your own priorities and practices around the questions they are grappling with here as we, together, strive to fulfill the mandate set out for us by Ms. Fichandler in her testimony: the American Theater as an instrument of our civilization.

Polly K. Carl
Director, Center for the Theater Commons, Emerson College
Editor, HowlRound | HowlRound.com

David Dower
Director of Artistic Programs
ArtsEmerson: The World On Stage

EXECUTIVE SUMMARY

On November 4–5, 2011, twenty-five theater professionals gathered in Washington, DC, for a meeting, hosted by the American Voices New Play Institute (AVNPI) at Arena Stage, to discuss nonprofit and commercial collaborations aimed at the development of new theatrical work.[1] In spirit (if not structure and size) the meeting represented the third installment of an ongoing conversation that was sparked in June 1974 when 224 representatives from the American theater gathered at Princeton University to entertain the (then) remote possibility of cooperation between the nonprofit and commercial theater in the interest of advancing the American stage. The 1974 convening was highly contentious and more than a quarter of a century would pass before another would be scheduled. By the time the conversation was rekindled in 2000, and a comparably constituted group gathered at Harvard University, much had changed: once unlikely alliances with commercial producers had become business-as-usual for a number of nonprofit theaters.[2]

---

[1] At the time of this gathering, the inquiry into this intersection was housed in the American Voices New Play Institute at Arena Stage. Subsequently the program, staff, and the activities of the inquiry have moved to the Center for the Theater Commons at Emerson College.

[2] The First American Congress of Theater (FACT) and the second (ACT TWO) were documented in field publications. After the FACT: Conflict and Consensus is out of print, but generally available on Amazon.com. ACT TWO: A Report on the Second American Congress of Theater is available through the Theatre Communications Group publications catalogue.

While the first two gatherings were large assemblies, the one in 2011 was intentionally limited to a small number of people, the large majority of whom are directly involved in commercial nonprofit partnerships on a regular basis.[3] The primary goals of the meeting were (1) to understand how commercial/nonprofit partnerships—particularly those centered on the development of new work—had evolved in recent years; and (2) to discuss the impact of shifts in practice on those regularly engaged in collaborations. The size of the gathering was capped primarily by budgetary constraints as it was funded entirely by the AVNPI; however, it was also hoped that the size and makeup of the group would encourage a forthright conversation and provide the time and space for participants to thoughtfully discuss complex issues.

To understand the significance of the 2011 meeting it is perhaps helpful to get a sense of what transpired at the 1974 and 2000 meetings.

FACT: June 1974

The aim of the organizers of the First American Congress of Theater (FACT) in 1974 was to bring the leaders of the American theater together to address a number of problems that could "no longer be dealt with effectively by any one segment of the community," including declining attendance and the need to stimulate youth and minority audiences, an economic recession, rising operating and production costs, and unreliable financing (Little 1975, 7). The meeting was initiated by the commercial theater, whose finances and audiences had been deteriorating over the previous three seasons. Broadway producers wanted to see if (then) seemingly more prosperous nonprofit theaters would be willing to come together to discuss the problems facing the American theater and consider ways of working together to address them (what many nonprofits took to mean joint lobbying for subsidies or more favorable tax policies for the commercial theater industry).

---

[3]Six commercial producers, ten representatives from nonprofit theaters (of which, four from Arena Stage), five artists, and four with other roles in the theater industry. Some individuals have crossed between categories over the course of their careers; people are categorized based on their current roles.

By all accounts, the 1974 meeting would have made for great reality television. Chairs were thrown, people threatened to storm out of the room, voices were raised, and insults were hurled. If the commercial theater came to test the waters for collaboration, it seems the nonprofit theater showed up to meet the enemy eye-to-eye and decline the offer (albeit some more diplomatically than others). As Richard Schechner (theater director and scholar) scoffed, "Do we want to lend support to subsidizing a system which many of us oppose? ... Why torpedo a ship for ten years, and then when it is going down help to rescue it?" (Little 1975, 52)

Though things would begin to unravel for the resident theater movement within a few years, in 1974 it was still confident and idealistic. An alternative theatrical arena with alternative financing, goals, and values had been successfully created and it was gaining legitimacy. Broadway was no longer the only (or even preferred) destination for new work. Aside from the clear ambitions to align interests on the part of the commercial producers, what emanates most from the report on the 1974 meeting is the sense that nonprofit theaters were still actively defining themselves in opposition to the commercial theater.

ACT TWO: June 2000

In 2000, a second meeting of nonprofit and commercial theaters was organized (this time by Theatre Communications Group with the League of American Theatres and Producers) and held at the American Repertory Theater at Harvard University.[4] In the extended hiatus between the two assemblies, once improbable collaborations between commercial producers and nonprofit theaters had "become so commonplace," it was "hard to find anyone able to work up a full dander

---

[4]Theatre Communications Group is the national service organization for nonprofit theaters. The League of American Theatres and Producers (now called the Broadway League) is a trade association for commercial theaters and producers. American Repertory Theater is a nonprofit theater founded by Robert Brustein.

about the subject anymore." (Gerard 2002, 9) Why had nonprofit theaters succumbed to the advances of the commercial theater, after all? In an essay published in advance of the convening, "Broadway: Devil or Angel for Nonprofit Theater? Finding the Right Way to Cross the Divide," Ben Cameron, then executive director of Theatre Communications Group, cited as causes the "drastic diminution of public subsidy since the Reagan years," "the unreliability of sustained foundation support," and the encouragement of "alliances" by foundations and others.

While the atmosphere was generally conciliatory, with both sides focusing on points of alignment rather than dissension, there were still a few voices in the room warning that commercial partnerships were having, or would have over time, a corrupting influence on nonprofits. Peter Schneider (then of Walt Disney Studios) asserted, "We bring shows to the not-for-profit and change the artistic mission of the companies." Likewise, (then) commercial producer Rocco Landesman tried to provoke debate by asking, "What *is* the mission of the nonprofit sector, of the subsidized theater? Are these theaters now simply Broadway tryout houses where we Broadway producers bring our products to get developed, or at the same time do they become Broadway producers themselves, setting up shop on Broadway, becoming virtually undistinguishable from us Broadway production companies?" (Gerard 2002, 45)

However, those concerned with the erosion of the nonprofit mission seemed to be outnumbered and unable to persuade others in the room that there were serious reasons to worry. Toward the end of the convening, commercial producer Jack Viertel, who was on the steering committee and helped to plan the event, remarked that he had "learned a couple of important things" from the three-day discussion:

> [The first is] that the battle between the commercial theater and the not-for-profit theater in terms of collaboration is a bankrupt idea for a panel and that there *is* no battle. The second ... is that the argument that the resident theater has betrayed its mission by

> collaborating with the commercial[5] theater is at the very least an argument that cannot be ignited in this room. It's been tried and it hasn't worked. Maybe if Bob Brustein had not fled to Italy it would have been easier to ignite. But it seems as though we all seem to be on the same side here and no one seems to feel that missions have been betrayed. And I think that's wonderful. (Gerard 2002, 68)

While there was, evidently, "no battle," Ben Cameron observed in his closing remarks that there was a "consistent tension" that had not been fully explored by the group—a "division of values or motives." Cameron noted that hearing another participant talk about the distinction between "product" and "process" prompted his own reflection that "even though we are after the same final purpose, maybe we have different reasons to get there." (Gerard 2002, 77–78)

It's fair to say that the underexplored terrain noted by Cameron (having to do with purpose, process, values, and motives) was decently plumbed at the third meeting in 2011. It's perhaps worth noting that Bob Brustein was present for the entire discussion.[6]

In the Intersection: November 2011

> What I'm trying to say is that there are certain *ideals* that were *constructed* for the nonprofit theater, which I have not heard a word about in the last two days. We all deviate from the ideals—ideals are meant to deviate from. But you have to know what they are in order to deviate from them. And what I'm not hearing is the fact that there *was* a time when we were *different theaters*, we did *different*

---

[5] The original transcript and report on the ACT TWO convening reads "collaborating with the not-for-profit theater;" however, Mr. Viertel confirmed in an email with the author that this was a misstatement, he intended to say "commercial" theater; and the phrase could be modified in this report.
[6] Bob Brustein is the founder of ART and Yale Repertory Theatre and one of the more vocal critics of commercial enhancement deals.

> things. We didn't join together to do the same things to please the largest number, to bring in the greatest amount of money, and the greatest subscribers. We did, as a nonprofit theater, most of us did these things because nobody else would do them!—Bob Brustein

If there was a recurring theme to the 2011 discussion, it was that the nonprofit theater appears to have lost sight of its values and *raison d'être*. While commercial partnerships were not perceived to be the cause of this erosion of ideals, necessarily, participants acknowledged that commercial transfers from nonprofits have increased in frequency (within organizations and across the field) and—along with box office success, reviews in *The New York Times*, enhancement income, royalties, Tony awards, working with celebrities, and the other "bells and whistles" associated with them—have become increasingly important measures of success at many LORT theaters.[7]

Collaborations and partnerships were generally considered to be beneficial by the group, with both commercial and nonprofit producers acknowledging that there is work that would not be created were it not for these partnerships. At the same time, concerns were expressed. Among them, that the goals and values of nonprofit and commercial producers can be at odds; that costs and risks associated with enhancement deals are escalating; that artists are often put in the position of serving two masters; that the prospects of a Broadway run can change the artistic process and product; and that such partnerships have the potential to create a legal and moral slippery slope for nonprofits.

If there was a clarion call from the meeting, it was perhaps for clarification around this moral line—what some called the *value proposition* of resident theaters. There was a sense that regional theaters have

---

[7]League of Resident Theaters is a professional theater association made up of seventy-five member theaters (as of 2012). LORT administers the primary national not-for-profit collective bargaining agreements with Actors' Equity Association, the Stage Directors and Choreographers Society, and United Scenic Artists.

been, to some greater or lesser degree, falling down on their watch—not providing adequate support to artists; not taking the artistic risks that they were created to take; not existing first and foremost for their local communities; and, most of all, not upholding alternative measures of success and an alternative set of values to those upheld by the commercial theater. While there was agreement that a larger shift in the values of the culture at large has created an environment increasingly less supportive of the nonprofit theater and that, in many ways, the nonprofit theater has simply turned toward the market (by necessity) along with the rest of the culture—there was also a pervasive sentiment that the nonprofit theater, if it is to have a purpose distinct from the commercial theater, needs to reclaim its lost identity.

***

While there was a loose structure to the two-day meeting, and various moderators endeavored to point participants in one direction or another, the conversation was allowed to flow where it wanted, which was, quite often, to a rather existential place. Participants reflected on such questions as: Where are we and how did we get here? What is the shape of the intersection between the two sectors—is it a crossroads or two lanes merging on a highway (as two participants debated)? Are we really *partners*—is that the right word to describe the relationship in the philosophical or legal sense? Is the partnership equal? Are the goals, processes, and values of partners in conflict, aligned, or perhaps too aligned? When collaborations work, why do they work? What goes wrong in the intersection? Can we fix what's not working or are such issues inevitable given our differences? For that matter, are we still different theaters, or have lines become too blurred? Do we need ethical guidelines governing work in the intersection? Is a firewall needed? What would we lose if these partnerships went away?

The many issues raised by the group seemed to cluster into four topics, broadly speaking: (1) What brings producers and nonprofits into the intersection? (2) Where are the collisions in the intersection? (3) Is it

IN THE INTERSECTION

an intersection, or is it a merger? That is, do nonprofit theaters still have a distinctive value proposition? (4) Where do we go from here?

What Brings Commercial Producers and Nonprofits into the Intersection?

> There's this Yale *Theater* 1979 issue, which is something about, "Why has the nonprofit theater failed us?" ... And the preface of the whole thing is by Ruth Mayleas, who was the first theater program officer at the NEA. And she said that what we're watching is the starving of something that started with a promise: that the Ford Foundation laid the seed work, and in a conversation between important people of this country, the Endowment was born to take up the gauntlet. *That never happened!* By 1979 ... we were already eating ourselves to stay alive. And to find we were making it up! I mean, I wasn't there, I can't say "we"; they were making it up as they went along. And the choice at the time, I think, was pretty stark and I think it remains: you either do this, or you're gone. And the trick becomes, how do you do it with integrity and without losing your purpose and vision? And I think we must understand that that kind of theater we're talking about—the bold, brave, nurturing kind of theater—needs to be supported massively and this is not what this culture's going to do. It's just not going to do it.—Jim Nicola

In reviewing the history of the resident theater movement, participants agreed (along the lines of Ben Cameron in 2000) that it was, in large part, financial necessity on both sides that first drove the commercial and nonprofit theater together. While there are many examples (going back to the 60s and 70s) of nonprofits self-producing works on Broadway or producing works that were subsequently transferred to Broadway by a commercial producer, in the 80s (when the rug was pulled out from under the nonprofit theater, as one participant suggested) a new type of deal emerged—which some participants perceive to have represented a "sea change" for the theater field.

In response to rising production costs and other forces, commercial producers needed to find an alternative to the commercial out-of-town tryout, or Off-Broadway run—their historic avenues for developing and test marketing new properties (mostly musicals). They began approaching nonprofit theaters, many of which by then had significant artistic and operational capacity, to see if they would fill this role—offering in exchange royalties and funds to cover the incremental costs associated with producing the works (later called "enhancement"). Around this same time, the implicit partners of the resident theater movement (private foundations and the NEA) began to pull their financial support just as growth in the size of venues and operating budgets at many theaters necessitated that they dramatically *increase* both revenues and audiences.

Participants from nonprofit theaters remarked that without the influx of royalties and enhancement income, in combination with other sources of support, it would not have been possible for them to sustain costume and scene shops, support the development of new work, and keep their institutions afloat these many years. But money was not then (nor is it now) the only, or even necessarily the primary motivation for nonprofit theaters and commercial producers to partner. As one producer noted, commercial producers often have the rights to properties that nonprofits would like to produce and resident theaters have large subscription and single ticket audiences, which producers need in order to test works and take them to the next level. Also significant, the conversation revealed that many partnerships seem to grow out of personal relationships or through a mutual passion for an artist or a project. (Notably, some of the commercial producers to first approach nonprofits in the 80s came from the nonprofit realm and, thus, were friends with the leaders of nonprofits and had shared tastes or aesthetics.)

But in looking for reasons for the increasing frequency of these deals over the past two decades (in smaller nonprofits as well as larger ones) all of these factors seemed to pale in comparison to one noted repeatedly by the group: the social and political shifts in the culture-at-large. The resident theater movement was formed at a time when society was supportive of its alternative, socialist, and collectivist ideals and, in the 80s, when the larger culture began to turn away from those ideals and towards more market-oriented ones, so did the American theater. As The Public Theater's artistic director, Oskar Eustis, described it (at two different points in the conversation):

> This has nothing to do with just the arts, or just theater. It's that the entire culture started swinging to the right in the Carter administration and kept going and kept going. ... Everybody understood that there were socialist values, there were union values, there were labor-should-be-in-power values, there were redistribution-of-wealth values that had a significant role in the dialogue of the culture. And that is just totally different now.

> The nonprofit theater is supposed to be a theater driven by values that are not determined by the marketplace. The commercial theater is supposed to be determined by the marketplace. That's the difference between the two. But it seems to me that we are operating within a cultural climate where the sources of support that are (again, throughout the culture) separate from the market, have been reduced dramatically.

This ideological shift was perceived variously by participants to have been manifested in the changing expectations and behaviors of foundations, government agencies, audiences, individual donors, the press, and board members, as well as by the growing power of the managing director in nonprofit theaters, relative to the artistic director. Nonprofit producers acknowledged that, over time, the metrics of success within their organizations began to shift. As Mara Isaacs at the McCarter Theatre said:

> What I have seen at more than one theater is this sort of growth, the definition of success, morphing. ... And this transactional culture that we're all moving toward, whether we like it or not, *that*

is becoming the predominant lens through which the conversations about the vision of the organization [are] happening

Some nonprofits commented that even if subsidies were increased to the point where they were no longer dependent on commercial partnerships for income, they would still engage in them because of the validation (and other critical resources) they now bring to their institutions.

Having said this, financial issues still loom large. There was consensus that the current economic model for both the nonprofit and commercial theater is broken. As Tony Taccone of Berkeley Rep rather dramatically described the situation, "Now, listen, we're here together because we were on two different ships, they both hit icebergs, and we both jumped into the same life raft. We find ourselves in the same life raft together." Producer Kevin McCollum suggested the problem is that nonprofit and commercial theaters are research and development enterprises (like pharmaceutical companies) but have been operating like manufacturing firms. There was universal agreement with his suggestion that the two sectors "need a new toolbox." And on an industry level, many lamented the loss of commercial Off-Broadway and noted the critical space between the regions and Broadway that it once filled.

Finally, both commercial and nonprofit producers remarked that there is work that simply would not be ventured were it not for these partnerships and that often they need each other to take a work or an artist to the next level of development. As one commercial producer said, "The reality is we need each other to do *anything*—to do *anything* now."

Where Are the Collisions in the Intersection?

David Dower: There's something disquieting about something going on here. And the disquieting thing is what I'm trying to get us to find.

Edgar Dobie: Well, David, our experiences in this intersection have been head-on collisions.

IN THE INTERSECTION

Two basic types of deals were discussed by the participants: (1) those initiated by commercial producers who have the relationship to an artist, or property rights, and who are seeking a nonprofit theater at which to do a pre-Broadway tryout or a developmental production; (2) those initiated by nonprofits that have the relationship to an artist, or property rights, and who are seeking a commercial partnership to support the development of a work and/or a Broadway transfer of a work once it is completed. Either type of deal may involve the exchange of property rights or income from enhancement or royalties.

When prompted to consider how and why things go wrong in the intersection, participants noted a range of concerns, but three that captured the most attention were artistic control, loyalty to project versus community, and the impact of the partnerships on the artistic process and product.

Artistic control:
Not surprisingly, a key issue that arises in the intersection surrounds the area of artistic control. Repeatedly, the conversation revealed that the party that initiates the deal typically seeks to exercise some level of creative control throughout the process. How much and over what areas differ by deal. Some commercial producers are said to "move in" and exert considerable control when they have originated and enhanced a production, while others are perceived to be more "hands off" (although the consensus by the group was that commercial producers are rarely, if ever, completely hands off). Many producers say they are aiming for "partnership" with the nonprofit, a term which seems to suggest shared control. As commercial producer Margo Lion remarked:

> It's important for a commercial producer to select [a nonprofit to work with] not just according to who has an open *slot*, and who has an appropriate space, and who has money (which, of course, is always a concern); but rather, who is going to be your ... *creative partner* in this?

At a minimum, commercial producers acknowledged that if they have originated and financed a production (in part or full) they will often seek to attach key members of the creative team to the project up front, before contracts are signed, and to obtain agreement from the nonprofit partner that approval will be sought before making changes to the creative team during the production process. While such concessions are noted to have become standard in partnership agreements, they are also a reason some nonprofits are reluctant to engage in deals that are initiated by commercial producers: they do not want to be in a position of losing control over the creative team and process.

Oskar Eustis admitted that the scenario in which a commercial producer brings a project to a nonprofit felt like "a line" for him, "a threshold" he would not cross. He elaborated:

> Actually, my feeling when I run institutions is that I've been invested with a great charge, which is the husbandry and stewardship of an institution that is fundamentally belonging to the community. It belongs to everybody. That's why it has a 501(c)(3). It has a 501(c)(3) because nobody but the people own it. And theoretically, what my job is, is to *defend* that mission, to *align* with that mission. … But I realize why I've never crossed that line. I can't imagine putting a show on in one of my theaters that I'm not responsible for the artistic choices.

It would become increasingly clear over the course of the two days that negotiating artistic control, no matter which party originates the deal, or whether or not enhancement is involved, can be tricky. In part this is because both parties, nonprofit and commercial producers, often (though not always) want to have a producing role: they both want to *make the work* and both have aesthetic preferences for how it should be made and marketed. Commercial producers, contrary to perhaps popular belief, do not want to be relegated to the role of "bank" any more than resident theaters want to be relegated to the role of "venue."

As commercial producer Michael David put it:

> I never really thought when we went to someone and said, "*Into the Woods* is really good" that what they saw was a dollar sign when we walked in.
>
> The fact is *we got good ideas too*! And so we found people that wanted to share those good ideas; and the fact that we were from different institutions or different places, became incidental. Now, I couldn't be more afraid of what's happening out there. I'm a passionate theater person more than anything else and I look to the nonprofit to do the things we can't possibly dare to do in that stupid place we work. But please don't minimize our passion, insight, perhaps even taste, by suggesting that if we happen to bring it to you there's got to be something wrong with it.

Matters surrounding artistic control are also complicated because a nonprofit theater could, theoretically, jeopardize its nonprofit status if it were to lose the ability to control how it spends its resources or (in essence) turn itself into a laboratory for commercial producers. While no one suggested that this was happening at any nonprofits, attorney John Breglio cautioned the group that these areas can be a slippery slope. While artistic control is generally covered in the contracts for commercial/nonprofit deals, the conversation also revealed that partners sometimes eschew contracts and rely on trust for as long as possible. While this is perceived by many to aid the partnership, it can also expose one or both parties to risks if conflicts arise or if deals fall apart—both of which happen.

Loyalty to project vs. local community:
On the subject of conflicts, several participants noted that disagreements can develop over how to proceed when a key member of the creative team is lost or a project is not coming together financially or artistically. While a commercial producer's preferred strategy in such a situation is frequently to postpone, resident theaters are often reluctant to cancel a show once it has been publicly announced and would prefer to make whatever changes are necessary and press forward. Some perceive such

conflicts to be symptomatic of the fact that the primary relationships and goals of commercial producers and nonprofits are fundamentally at odds.

At the point at which they intersect with a nonprofit theater, commercial producers are generally on a multiyear arc with an artist/project in which they have already invested considerable time and money. Their investment is in the long-term success of the product and, often, the generative artists on the creative team.

As commercial producer Kevin McCollum remarked:

> Commercial producers are developing, much more perhaps than the not-for-profits realize and we are looking [out] for the whole life of that show, and for as long as possible. And, actually, our primary relationship is with the *author*. ... We're looking at hopefully a decade relationship with this project.

Nonprofits, on the other hand, generally have the primary goal of ensuring the longevity and well-being of their institutions, which requires safeguarding their reputations and relationships with their subscribers, the local press, and other key community stakeholders.

Edgar Dobie of Arena Stage described the difference saying:

> We actually convince them to spend eight or ten ... or twelve evenings with us. And we take that responsibility very seriously. And so when we put something on the playbill, we're actually driven by an imperative, which commercial producers are not always driven by, which is, "The show will go on and we will deliver the show."

Deals frequently "fall off the map." While some collapse before they have been publicly announced, the risks for a nonprofit that loses a show from its season once it has already been sold to subscribers and announced to the local press can be devastating. As one artistic director commented to another participant, "How do we as a not-for-profit theater protect ourselves from this kind of thing? How do we protect ourselves? ... Because it's *our* audiences and *our* local press?"

IN THE INTERSECTION

Impact on the process and product:
Another significant thread of the conversation concerned the fact that even when there is shared alignment around the goal (trying to create great work), conflicts can arise because of divergent values and processes.

As Tony Taccone remarked:

> There's a systemic issue, I think, in terms of how groups of people come together and interact. And what are the values that actually drive those collaborations? Obviously there's a shared project, which everybody believes in. Now, one thing I want to say is that my experience of working with people from the [commercial] world ... has been largely positive. I've been impressed with how smart they are, how committed they are. *But* the values that they are pursuing are not entirely the same as the values that Berkeley Rep is pursuing as an institution and the way we organize people around it.

Many participants noted that the creative team can be put in the position of serving two masters (that is, negotiating input from both the commercial and nonprofit producers). Moreover, there was general agreement among the nonprofit theaters that once it is known that a piece will move to Broadway it can influence the artists and the work itself.

From Jim Nicola:

> I think the problem is that when you take enhancement money inside the imagination of the artist something occurs. That they are headed in a certain direction with certain formal demands that are inescapable.

Molly Smith at Arena Stage agreed saying:

> I think what you're saying is absolutely right, Jim. What happens in that case, as soon as people who are within the cast, or within the creative team, feel this sense of "and now it may go on," it changes. It changes.

And producer Michael David suggested repeatedly that having a fixed date on Broadway is the "great adulterator" of deals and poisons relationships.

On the whole, artists in the room were quite positive about their experiences working in the commercial realm. They noted that it is where they make the most money, achieve greater visibility and recognition, and also that relationships with commercial producers are often more transparent and less ambiguous than those with nonprofit producers. On the other hand, both nonprofit and commercial producers agreed that Broadway can be incredibly brutal for writers. Taking playwrights from the regions to Broadway was said to be akin to "taking them into a snake pit," "driving them into the buzz saw of capitalism," or "throwing them to the wolves."

A related area of concern (also thought to be increasing risks and affecting the creative process) was the press. Commercial producers often take shows to nonprofits looking for a safe place to try out the work; however, sometimes because they are invited by the regional theaters, and sometimes because they buy tickets even when they are not invited, the national press is increasingly inclined to cover these premieres. This increased press attention is perceived to be eroding the historic "safe environment" that nonprofits were once able to provide to artists and projects (both those done in partnership with commercial producers and not).

Intersection or Merger? Do Nonprofit Theaters Still have a Distinctive Value Proposition?

> What's missing today is the subsidy that allows these people to do the things they want. They're naturally falling back on box office. It's inevitable to do that. Or to get enhancement money that's going to flow to the theater and allow that play to go to Broadway where it will always be a pot of gold as *Chorus Line* was to Joe.[8] That's understandable.

---

[8] Referring to Joseph Papp, founding artistic director of The Public Theater, producer of *A Chorus Line*.

IN THE INTERSECTION

> It's almost as if everyone has to have one of these. But then you get the taste of it in your mouth and you want more of it. And gradually you're growing out of your old commitment to a collective ideal, your idealism, and you're becoming—essentially, whether you know it or not, you're becoming a Broadway producer.—Bob Brustein

One of the more provocative ideas running across the two days concerned the erosion of the nonprofit value proposition. About midway through the second day Polly Carl reflected on the discussion thus far saying, "I'm so struck by the need for the not-for-profit to just get their house in order and decide what their value proposition is." Others agreed, including Oskar Eustis who remarked:

> [G]ood fences make good neighbors. I think if our house is clear, if our house is clean, it's going to be much easier for us to have a very productive relationship with our commercial friends, because it will be clear what we do and it will be clear what they do and we'll feel what our common ground is and we'll make appropriate contracts and we'll be rewarded for it.

Many noted that it is no longer evident what value nonprofits bring to the table, distinct from commercial producers. Some suggested that the interests of nonprofit and commercial producers are now aligned to the point where the shape of the intersection is less like a crossroads and more like two lanes merging on the highway. While nonprofits and commercial producers are supposed to have different missions (and perhaps do), participants noted that they are more and more the same in practice. Conflicts may now be arising, some thought, not because values are clashing in the intersection, but because the purposes of commercial producers and nonprofits have become *too* aligned—both are creating similar work and both see their role as one of research and development. In other words, they may be competing to occupy the same space.

Some expressed a concern that programming across resident theaters (both those engaged in commercial partnerships and not) is increasingly homogenous and commercial: that theaters are losing their regional identities and programming works that have been successful elsewhere (more often than not, New York) rather than creating work for and with their local communities.

Over the course of the two days, many wondered whether resident theaters have begun to lose sight of their purpose, their values, and their artistic and social missions, and have, instead, begun to adopt commercial values and measures of success. While participants were adamant that tax laws need not be changed to address these issues, Oskar Eustis floated the idea that perhaps influential funders could draw a line in the sand and offer support only to those theaters operating on the right side of the line (much as W. McNeil Lowry at the Ford Foundation did at the formation of the resident theater movement in 1959).

Recognizing that the metrics of success and the values of nonprofits have changed is one thing. Changing them back is quite another. Towards the end of the two-day convening, commercial producer David Binder asked, "How can we create success for artists that is not contextualized on whether the show moves to Broadway?" No answer was forthcoming.

Along the same lines, composer Michael Friedman challenged the room to think of a non-commercial Off-Broadway musical that had not moved to Broadway in the past eight to ten years that was considered to be a great success. After a long silence Margo Lion said, "You can't do it anymore." A couple of productions were mentioned but it was agreed that these were exceptions that proved the rule. A bit later, in reference to the incredible success of *Rent*, Friedman remarked:

> I got to New York in 1997 and for all of us who got to New York after *Rent* opened on Broadway, it was a changed landscape. Probably only *Hair* and *Chorus Line* changed the landscape as much, in the sense of changing the entire expectation level of everything.... So, in a funny way, I would say "enhancement shmenhancement"—it's almost like because of that show if you write a musical and are at a not-for-profit, if you do not go to the Nederlander

and run for seven years, twelve years, fifteen years, you've failed. ... The definition of success—that's transformed for all of us.

Where Do We Go From Here?

> Things have become blurred and muddled and the mission has diffused largely because of exigencies, realities, necessities. But it seems to me, more than anything else, what the not-for-profit sector, what the resident theater sector can use more than anything else, is a kind of booster shot of idealism.—Rocco Landesman

For the last session of the day, participants were invited to reflect on what might be included in a statement of ideals or principles that could serve as a guidepost for collaborations in the intersection between the nonprofit and commercial theater. After taking time to reflect on the question, participants shared their recommendations, which seemed to be of four types: those seeking to require nonprofits to do more for artists; those seeking to require nonprofits to do more for their communities; those encouraging nonprofits to clarify their purpose or mission; and those seeking to restrict nonprofits from engaging in activities that would compromise their mission. Here are some of the ideas that emerged from the exercise:

> **The commercial and nonprofit theater have common priorities: artist support, long-term development of new work, and audiences for that work. The two sectors need to work toward transparency around expectations, examining definitions of "success," strengthening tolerance for risk, and more clearly defining the research and development, manufacturing, and distribution processes at the intersection.** —Sue Frost

> **An imperative to grow the audience demographic because this country is changing and we will not have anyone going to the theater if we don't make that a top concern.** —Margo Lion

There needs to be something about the mutual building of community—meaning commercial producers should not simply fly in and fly out without taking an interest in the community. —Molly Smith

What nonprofits really need are ethics statements. —Polly Carl

Institutions need to reinvest in, refine, and articulate their institutional purpose and vision with an understanding of their personal definition of success; to resist the inexorable pull of market forces; and to reestablish themselves as community leaders, as places that sustain artists, and as places to express a core set of values. —Mara Isaacs

Nonprofit organizations should lead their buildings: meaning, buildings should serve organizations rather than organizations serve buildings. —David Binder

Don't let anyone get between you and the relationship with the writer. —Edgar Dobie

In the end, there was never consensus on the shape of the intersection; however, there was consensus that these partnerships need to serve the long-term missions of nonprofits as much or more than they serve other short-term ends and that, in order for that to happen, attention needs to be paid to reaffirming or strengthening the values and purposes of nonprofit theaters, separate from commercial theaters. There was a sense that this was an important conversation and that the blurring of the lines between the commercial and not-for-profit theater, though perhaps inevitable to some degree, is disconcerting and requires deeper examination because these deals are done in the intersection between two sectors that are (or perhaps should be) driven by different goals, processes, and values.

The Structure of This Report

The first day of the convening was structured around four panel discussions. Each session began as a conversation between a few participants, but then quickly opened up to a full group discussion. The first two sessions brought a historical perspective to the discussion. Gregory Mosher and Rocco Landesman were brought together to discuss what had changed since Landesman's 1988 diatribe against some of the practices of Mosher (and his then partner Bernard Gersten) when they were running Lincoln Center Theatre.[9] Mosher, in particular, stimulated a provocative discussion by acknowledging that his views on the issues raised in Landesman's rant in *The New York Times* had changed because he had seen the impact of commercial behavior on the ethos and aims of nonprofit theaters. This perspective was furthered as Oskar Eustis and Robert (Bob) Brustein reflected on the formation of the resident theater movement, what it was seeking to achieve, and why it began to stumble. The third session centered on contracts, the various points of negotiation in commercial/nonprofit partnerships, and how deals have changed over time. And the fourth session featured a panel discussion with the three playwrights-in-residence at Arena Stage, which sought to bring forward perspectives of artists on work in and between the two sectors. On the second day, participants were encouraged to reflect on "where things go wrong" in the intersection. The format was three small group discussions (commercial producers, nonprofit producers, and artists/artist representatives), followed by breakout sessions, which were followed by two full group discussions.

In an effort to provide a setting conducive for any concerns to be openly discussed, participants were told that the 2011 meeting would not be open to the press.[10] Unfortunately, barring the press elicited a bit

---

[9]http://www.nytimes.com/1988/12/11/theater/theater-what-price-success-at-lincoln-center.html?pagewanted=all&src=pm
[10]The organizers of the 1974 meeting also wanted a closed-door session but were persuaded to allow press to attend the event on a limited basis. Virtually the entire 2000 meeting was closed to journalists, with the exception of Jeremy Gerard, the journalist/writer hired to document the conference for the record.

of a backlash from at least one journalist, as well as some theater practitioners, for diverse reasons, including the perception that the action was in conflict with the AVNPI policy of "radical transparency" with its proceedings (which heretofore, had been streamed on the Internet in an effort to make it possible for anyone interested in the discussions to observe and participate).[11] Nonetheless, it was ultimately determined that inviting the press after having promised the participants that the press would not be present would compromise the integrity and aims of the meeting, and it was closed. In writing the summary report of the discussion, great efforts have been made to let the participants speak for themselves and to accurately convey the key points of each conversation without betraying confidences or potentially harming any individuals or institutions. Additionally, while endeavoring to stay true to the overall arc of each session, comments have been grouped by topic area for the purposes of highlighting significant themes. Thus, in some cases, comments are presented out of chronological sequence.

Diane Ragsdale is currently working towards a PhD at Erasmus University in Rotterdam. Her subject is the resident theater movement in the United States and the evolution in its relationship to the commercial theater over the past thirty years. For the six years prior to transitioning to academia, Ragsdale worked in the Performing Arts Program of The Andrew W. Mellon Foundation, where she had primary responsibility for theater and dance grants. Before joining the Foundation, Diane served as managing director of the performing arts center On the Boards in Seattle. Prior work also includes stints at several film, music, and arts festivals. She is a frequent speaker at arts conferences within and outside of the United States. She holds an MFA in acting and directing from University of Missouri Kansas City and a BFA in theater and BS in psychology from Tulane University.

---

[11] Peter Marks from the Washington Post challenged the decision of Arena Stage to ban the press in his article, "Arena Stage Bans Media, Public from New-Play Conference." Available at: http://www.washingtonpost.com/lifestyle/style/arena-stage-bans-media-public-from-new-play-conference/2011/11/02/gIQAqAhOmM_story.html

DAY 1
HISTORICAL VIEWPOINTS:
Rocco Landesman and Gregory Mosher

Moderated by Diane Ragsdale

> You know what? From the perspective of twenty years later, you were absolutely right.—Gregory Mosher (to Rocco Landesman)

The 2011 meeting examining the intersection between the commercial and nonprofit theater was set to begin with a conversation between Rocco Landesman, current Chairman of the National Endowment for the Arts (NEA), and theater producer and director Gregory Mosher. All present had witnessed firsthand, or read in the packet of materials sent in advance of the meeting, the lashing in the Arts section of *The New York Times* that Landesman had given Mosher (and his then business partner, Bernard Gersten) nearly twenty-five years earlier, when the former was still a Broadway producer and the latter two were running the nonprofit Lincoln Center Theater. Perhaps starting the meeting with a debate between these former jousting partners would ensure that the 2011 meeting would not be the nonevent that ACT II in 2000 was largely reported to be? One could sense hope on the part of at least a few in attendance that—as had occurred at the First American Congress of Theater in 1974, when the differences between nonprofits and commercial producers were still clear, important, and irreconcilable—a chair or two might be thrown. (Though hopefully not too forcefully given that the meeting was taking place in the glass-walled Molly Smith Library of the Mead Center for the Performing Arts, the newly expanded and renovated home of Arena Stage.)

As moderator for the first session, I began by reminding Landesman of some of the criticisms he had lobbed at Mosher and Gersten in his 1988 article, "What Price Success at Lincoln Center?"

> "The purpose of theater at Lincoln Center is to be successful" was one of your criticisms. You questioned, for instance, reviving *Anything Goes* and running it like a "cash cow." You noted that Lincoln Center was able to get special deals and concessions and salaries from union negotiations because of their nonprofit status. You said that Lincoln Center appeared to be a "magical kingdom," where theaters could morph from being nonprofit to being Broadway venues and back again to nonprofit venues, as suited the purpose at the time. You expressed fear that the "shocking, disturbing, and challenging work so vital to our culture would recede, inevitably, into the back of the repertory." And you said that "while the middle of the road might be a path to success, the theater might become a less exciting and ultimately less important place as a result of following that path." And you ended, asking ... "Why, Gregory Mosher and Bernard Gersten, are you doing theater at Lincoln Center?"

I gave Mosher the first opportunity to comment and asked him to reflect on his years at Lincoln Center Theater (LCT)—on what he was trying to achieve, and how the situation described by Landesman looked at the time from his perspective. Mosher characterized his move to LCT as a "fresh start." As is well known in American theater history, and as others would attest in this meeting, Mosher and Gersten came to turn on the lights at LCT after four years of darkness—a sufficient hiatus, it seems, to have allowed both the turmoil that had surrounded the theater in its early years ("a succession of unsuccessful regimes" as one participant would later characterize it) to diminish in potency. Mosher recounted:

So, we had a clean slate and I had been in Chicago for eleven years, and I wanted to start absolutely fresh. So, what we were pursuing was excellence, really.

Then the excellence became conflated with *success*, not necessarily in the sense that Rocco meant it, but in the *true* sense of success—that you invest everything you have in a play, and then it turns out that people like it! And that's a *good* thing it seems to me, in any context.

Mosher described the "true" success that he and Gersten were pursuing, and defended one of the works that Landesman had criticized in *The New York Times* article:

We got rid of subscription, which I've bored you all to tears with for twenty years, talking about how I think that's an anvil around the neck of any creative team. And we decided we would only do the things we really wanted to do and never devote any energy to "subscriber fodder." We did thirty-seven plays while we were there. About half of them were premieres. We did no workshops. We took no enhancement money. And we gambled with our own artists and our own people.

You know, Rocco is all over *Our Town* in that article and—fair enough. Except to me it was this great piece of art about World War II about to happen, written by a classics scholar who believed in 1939 in Europe, where he wrote that play, that this was the end of 2,500 years of the West. And he just *made* a small town in New Hampshire. Now, you just have to trust me, *that's* why I wanted to do the play. ...

I understand that people could think that was just cheesy pop crap. And doing art is kind of like Potter Stewart (from the high court) talking about pornography, "I can't define it, I just know it when I see it." And we all know art when we see it, but we can't define it. So we have to trust each other.

While comments like these peppered throughout Mosher's opening remarks may have suggested that he had come to this conversation at Arena Stage prepared to give a rebuttal to Landesman's 1988 article, it soon became clear that he had come to do the opposite. In the midst of a rather eloquent defense of LCT's artistic practices, Mosher stopped himself and said, "One of the reasons we (the three of us) are having this conversation is that at the Mellon I said [to Rocco], 'You know what? From the perspective of twenty years later, you were absolutely right.'"

Mosher then turned to me and asked, "Do you want me to say why I think Rocco was right ... or do you want me to wait on that?" I responded, "No, that's good." And Landesman added, "You're on a roll."

I interjected briefly to explain that in May 2010, when I was still working at The Andrew W. Mellon Foundation, we had invited Mosher, Landesman, and a few others to our offices for an informal meeting to discuss the relationship between the commercial and nonprofit theater and what had changed over the past thirty years. It was at that meeting that Mosher, holding the 1988 article in his hand (which he said he had read the night prior for the first time in years), turned to Landesman and said, "You were right." Landesman, as I recalled, responded, "I never thought I'd hear you say that."

The Problem is Shifting Measures of Success: Why Rocco was Right

I asked Mosher what he meant by the comment. He began, "My perspective was that I'd put my left hand on *Subscribe Now!* and raised my right hand to God and Peter Zeisler[12] and the Attorney General and said, "We're here to produce Art!" Mosher then suggested that when excellence leads to commercial success, and commercial success leads to

---

[12]Peter Zeisler, who died in 2005, was the co-founder of the Guthrie Theater and executive director of the Theatre Communications Group from 1972 to 1995.

"bells and whistles"—"the cash and the prizes and all the bullshit that theaters tell their boards about to get them excited to go out and raise more money"—then the bells and whistles themselves can become like a drug.

Mosher now perceives that Landesman accurately sensed not only that theaters might get hooked on the bells and whistles and forget about their institutional purpose "to create theatrical *art*," but could, and probably would, take shortcuts to obtain them. In other words, Landesman was concerned not only that nonprofits were crowding onto his commercial turf, but that nonprofits would eventually "start living a lie." Mosher continued:

> You would lie to your artists by saying they were central, but in fact pay them terribly and expect them to be the main subsidizing force in the American theater—probably in American arts. And you would lie to your board. And you would lie to your audience [by chasing "success" rather than excellence].

Mosher did not realize at the time (but now sees that Landesman did) that theaters could obtain the bells and whistles without addressing the components of LCT's strategies that Mosher saw as critical to its "true success" (or excellence) as a nonprofit professional theater. These strategies (which Mosher would reference over the course of the two days) included getting rid of subscription, paying decent wages to artists, not taking subsidiary rights from playwrights, providing adequate rehearsal time, and giving the artistic director complete control over what the theater did and how it did it.

A bit later Oskar Eustis, artistic director of The Public Theater, would ask Mosher to reflect a bit more on his use of the term "lie" and what had changed by the time he left LCT. After a pause, Mosher described no longer being able to have a conversation with people without being asked whether a show would run a long time. He said he perceived LCT's members were beginning to behave like subscribers and that there was a continual pressure to achieve success, but that success now meant *Sarafina!*, which ran for seven years.

Mosher later elaborated on the drug metaphor and clarified that he calls it a "drug" primarily because *institutions* become dependent on the rewards and legitimacy that accrue with commercial success; however, he acknowledged, and cajoled others into agreement, that individuals are not immune, saying:

> It's fun to park—you can't do it after 9/11—but it's fun to park in Shubert Alley or go to see Rocco at Jujamcyn. It's fun to sit in the fifth row on the aisle at the Tony awards. Your board members look at you in a different way. You know, a year ago you were a punk … [*laughter from the rest of the room*] … telling them they had absolutely no say about the theater. And then after they see you on TV they think you know something. You didn't know anything but now you're in your tuxedo! … So you, they, you get addicted to it.

I then asked Landesman to describe his perspectives (then and now) on the matter. It's fair to say that Landesman has been a consistent and vocal critic of commercial behavior in the nonprofit sector (both in his former life as a Broadway producer and in his current role as NEA chair)—this despite having instigated several commercial/nonprofit co-productions over the years, many of them stimulated by enhancement money. Landesman's party line on the matter has long been that commercial producers are not at fault for seeking to collaborate with nonprofits, but that regional theaters have the ethical responsibility to make choices that are in line with their nonprofit missions. Over the years, Landesman has repeatedly characterized the nonprofit theater as suffering from an "identity crisis." Landesman reminded those at Arena that the nonprofit theater was supposed to be an *alternative* to Broadway, to do *riskier* work not catering to the marketplace. He remarked that since the 70s he had been describing a seismic shift, a blurring of the lines between the sectors, the root cause of which he believed to be a cultural issue: changing definitions of success and a changing ethos. Landesman:

> ...At some point along the line, success became the driving
> concern and how you define success is critical to the whole
> thing. But by the time you got to the 1980s what everyone was
> interested in was doing well, was succeeding. The boards wanted
> this. The audiences all wanted the validation of the show before
> they saw it. Everybody wanted to be successful. And, of course,
> to the boards this always meant Broadway transfers or big box
> office or some kind of recognition in a national publication,
> whatever the metrics were. And there were always metrics.

One of the pioneers of the resident theater movement and the founder of the American Repertory Theater (at Harvard University) and Yale Repertory Theatre, Robert (Bob) Brustein, provided a historical perspective on the trap of success, saying:

> The geography of the American theater, which we're neglecting to
> talk about, is from idealism, obscurity, passion, commitment—what
> have you—to a certain modicum of fame, to being accepted
> and going after the next piece that's going to get you even more
> accepted. ... It happens to individuals. It happens to playwrights.

Brustein remarked on the career trajectory of Eugene O'Neill pointing out that after having started in an unknown, off-the-beaten-path theater (the Provincetown Players), then having had a string of plays on Broadway, O'Neill went back into obscurity in the 1930s and it was then that he wrote his best works (*Long Day's Journey Into Night*, *Moon for the Misbegotten*, *The Iceman Cometh*). Continuing to remind those in the room of their history and the lost ideals of the resident theater movement would prove to be one of Brustein's roles at this two-day meeting.

Landesman also pointed to a shift in the leadership structure of many nonprofit theaters as a contributing factor to the shifting measures of success—noting in particular the growing power of the managing director. He contrasted the current model to prior decades when artistic directors were often at the top of the organizational flow chart and managing directors or their equivalents held a supporting role, saying:

> Interestingly, in recent years, the managing director as, in effect, a representative of the board, has taken over more and more of the responsibility of the artistic work of the theater—to the point where you ... have evolved from *that* [referring to the old model with artistic director on top] to a coequal managing director and artistic director where you have an almost prescribed tension ... to the point now where, in effect, very often, the managing director is, in fact, the artistic director.

Brustein, as well, reflected on the inherent tension between artistic and managing partners and noted that after the success of *A Chorus Line* at The Public Theater, Michael Bennett (the creator of *A Chorus Line*) approached Joe Papp to produce his next work. Papp turned it down for artistic reasons, but Bernard Gersten (who managed the operations at The Public before going to LCT) disagreed with the decision. As Brustein said, "Bernie was the managing director and his impulse was to keep the theater solid. Joe was the artistic director; his impulse was to find exciting things." The disagreement over this issue, Brustein relayed, would eventually cause Papp and Gersten to part ways.

Brustein then made the link between the loss of support and the turn toward Broadway:

> What's missing today is the subsidy that allows these people to do the things they want. They're naturally going to fall back on box office. It's inevitable to do that. Or to get enhancement money that's going to flow to the theater and allow that play to go to Broadway where it will always be a pot of gold as *Chorus Line* was to Joe. That's understandable. It's almost as if everyone has to have one of these. But then you get the taste of it in your mouth and you want more of it. And gradually you're growing out of your old commitment to a collective ideal, your idealism,

and you're becoming—essentially, whether you know it or not, you're becoming a Broadway producer. And the big difference is that you're trying to please an audience and make money rather than please a group of artists, and an audience who are part of that artist collective, and make art. And that distinction gets lost. And once that's lost then we have this confusion of a misalliance between Broadway and nonprofit.

Kevin McCollum, a commercial producer who ran a nonprofit presenting venue for seven years, picked up on Brustein's comments about Papp and Gersten and pointed out that it was Gersten who had been instrumental in securing the capital from philanthropist Lou Esther Mertz (which Oskar Eustis pointed out was a *donation* and not a *loan*)—capital, as others noted, that allowed *A Chorus Line* to transfer and for The Public to reap the profits from its success and sow them back into producing new artists and new works. McCollum then commented wryly, "So here we are today. And it's just so interesting, the benevolence of *that* ... and then the *drug*. ... Now we have a bunch of drug dealers out there trying to make theater."

A bit later in the discussion Mara Isaacs, producer at the nonprofit McCarter Theatre, would suggest that the so-called drug problem was being misstated. She saw it from a slightly different angle. "There's this assumption that the problem is that all of these theaters all over the country are addicted to this heroin and living off of this commercial drug. I think the problem is that there are all these theaters around the country that would *like* to be addicted to heroin." Mosher agreed with Isaacs and said that this *was*, indeed, his point and also how he had interpreted Landesman's original concern in the 1988 article.

Several comments made over the course of the two days would suggest that both things were happening. On the one hand, shifting measures of success were affecting the entire field, not simply those that were actively co-producing with commercial partners or trying to move work to Broadway; and on the other, it seemed that a growing number of nonprofit theaters were also increasingly reliant upon commercial income and trying to create the next *Rent*, or *Chorus Line*, or *Jersey Boys*—despite the odds against replicating such successes.

Related to this, toward the end of the session Mosher would reference the book *Black Swan* by Nicholas Taleb, about the fallacy of prediction, commenting that while theater producers are "in the prediction business," Taleb's theory would suggest that "all of the interesting stuff (whether it's Harry Potter, or *A Chorus Line*)" is unlikely to be predicted by computer models or people working in institutions.

Ironically, despite this early contextualization of *Chorus Line*, *Rent*, and other such successes as being unpredictable, these productions and a few others (that are clearly watershed moments for the field) would be exhumed and examined more than a few times over the course of the two days for clues to their success.

The Problem is Money: The Resident Theater First Lost its Financial Partner Then its Ideals

A bit later Jim Nicola, artistic director of New York Theatre Workshop (NYTW), raised his hand and said, "I feel like we can't go forward without really clearly understanding how we got here. And I feel like we're missing something about this story or this myth of the past." Relaying ideas he recalled from a 1979 article in *Theater* magazine by Ruth Mayleas, first theater program officer at the NEA, Nicola said:

> And [Mayleas] said that what we're watching is the starving of something that started with a promise: that the Ford Foundation laid the seed work, and in a conversation between important people of this country, the Endowment was born to take up the gauntlet. *That never happened!* By 1979 ... we were already eating ourselves to stay alive. And to find we were making it up! I mean, I wasn't there, I can't say "we"; they were making it up as they went along. And the choice at the time, I think, was pretty stark and I think it remains: you either do this, or you're gone. And the trick becomes, how do you do it with integrity and without losing your purpose and vision? And I think we must understand that the

kind of theater we're talking about—the bold, brave, nurturing kind of theater—needs to be supported massively and this is not what this culture's going to do. It's just not going to do it.

There was a long silence. Brustein then pointed out that around this same time, the Ford and Rockefeller foundations had also pulled back their support of the arts and that only two major foundations continued to support theater: The Mellon and Shubert foundations (the latter, a private foundation started by the commercial theater producers of the same name). Brustein then compared Shubert's approach (channel profits into a foundation that supports nonprofit theaters) with the Merrick Foundation (started by commercial producer David Merrick), which would take profits and reinvest them directly in the production of new plays. He ended by commenting on the tremendous subsidies in Europe and reiterating his point that, given the NEA's insignificant level of support for most organizations (three to four percent of a theater's budget), it was inevitable for the artistic and managing directors to begin to look for other sources of income.

Michael David spoke, describing his transition from the nonprofit to commercial arena. David, along with Landesman, first studied theater at Yale Drama School under Bob Brustein; he and Landesman then went on to form a commercial production company, Dodger Theatricals.

> When we started, which was after graduating from Yale, ... we were in a free theater for five years. And then government funding went from $5,000 to $60,000 to $300,000. And if we were in Brooklyn, that was good enough to get a bigger grant! And then suddenly, these partners who were complicit in our existence, national and local governments, foundations—I mean you're on it! [*To Jim Nicola*] I mean, before we all drank the Kool-Aid (or some did and some didn't)—before the heroin of box office success—those complicit partners pulled out the rug. They abandoned us. Now, you know, in the end we just decided, "Hell, we're not going to go begging anymore." We turned to the dark side. [*Laughter*]

IN THE INTERSECTION

But there was this thing that happened. And I don't think it's because they looked around and saw that none of us were doing anything good and they decided not to give us any more money. They started something they couldn't finish and they went away.

The Problem is the Cultural Shift: The Alternative Ideology is Gone

Oskar Eustis chimed in with, "The whole *culture* did that!"—a comment which elicited affirmative nods and comments from across the room. Eustis elaborated saying that "the entire culture started swinging to the right during the Carter administration and kept going and kept going" and that the resident theater movement took for granted that there were values ("socialist, union, labor-should-be-in-power, redistribution-of-wealth values") that had "played a significant role in the dialogue of the culture" and that "it was different now."

Along these same lines, Bob Brustein raised a political issue that he felt was being neglected by the room. He commented, "One of the big differences between now and thirty, forty years ago, when Joe [Papp] was functioning" was that there was an "alternative ideology in the air, certainly through the 30s and it lasted through the 40s and 50s," and this "alternative ideology was the ideology of the collective." This is a topic to which Brustein and Eustis would return in the next session.

Eustis then responded to Brustein's heralding of countries providing significantly larger subsidies to the arts (than the United States does) and conveyed in disbelief that he (and others in the room) were now regularly asked to consult with theaters in other countries whose governments were telling them they needed to look to the United States as a model for how to support the arts. He ended by pulling together the three themes already on the table: the larger culture change, the loss of money, and the trap of success (the lure of the "drugs"):

…We should be clear that this [cultural shift] is not something that could be changed by a heroic Chairman of the NEA. …

> This is happening across the world. ... And there's a distinction that I just want to make really clear. There is the addiction. There is the drug. There is the fact that of course the Tony awards are fun, and the acclaim and all that. *That* temptation is a personal temptation that each of us has got to wrestle with; it's our job to wrestle with it. But there's also the question of the money, and following it, which is different. It's not about how tempting it is. It's about the fact that ... those of us who are charged with running institutions are charged with making those institutions succeed and be healthy—because if they aren't, no artists are going to get paid and no art is going to happen.

In the midst of Eustis's remarks, Gregory Mosher interjected to say that he saw the success (the drugs, the bells and whistles) as primarily a *corporate* temptation not a personal one, another topic that would re-emerge the second day within the context of the values and ethics of the nonprofit theater.

The Problem is Some Theaters Are Now Too Big to Fail: We Need a New Business Model

One of two attorneys in the room, John Breglio (who had recently transitioned from being an entertainment lawyer structuring deals for nonprofits and commercial entities to being a commercial producer), remarked that perhaps some American theaters "to borrow a phrase of today, become too big to fail. But as opposed to the federal government with the banks, we have nobody to bail us out." He suggested that we needed to distinguish between the largest theater institutions, especially those in New York, and the smaller regional theaters, some of which were still trying to hold up the ideals of the resident theater movement.

He returned to the subject of Joe Papp (whom he knew personally) and discussed what had changed since Papp's era: "*A Chorus Line* created the opportunity for Joe to never take, virtually ever, commercial money." That was not the situation, he said, for Papp's successors (George Wolfe and Oskar Eustis), who had to grapple with running a "huge institution that had to be fed" once the royalties had diminished. He suggested that the field may need to "rethink what these institutions have to be because they can't be fed any other way, I'm afraid, at this point in our culture, in this city, in this country—without this infusion of commercial money." Landesman responded glibly, "We had to turn to drugs because the culture was too painful." Breglio nodded in weary agreement and commented that once these institutions grow very large they are unsustainable and turn against you—that, in essence, they "become monsters."

Oskar Eustis remarked that the imperative for The Public to become as big as it had was so that it could provide work to artists and reach large audiences. He elaborated:

> ... the temptation about the commercial stuff, the genuine on-the-ground, daily pressure that I feel, is the pressure to maximize the audience and the income for the artists that have invested their years working with me. ... And that doesn't feel *bad*; that feels *right*. Unfortunately, the venue for it, the only real venue for it, is the commercial, which creates contradictions; but the alternative is *not* to simply tell everyone to start volunteering again and go make their living writing for TV.

Eustis soberly recounted that when he first came to The Public he spent time reviewing the commercial income the theater had received since 1972 (whether from royalties or enhancement) and that, in doing so, he learned that The Public had never been able to perform its mission without an infusion of income from the commercial sector. Eustis ended saying: "So, there's got to be a business model that deals with the reality of what we're in and doesn't just bemoan the fact that we're not in a different reality."

Likewise, commercial producer Sue Frost, who pushed throughout the two-days for a focus on solutions, would later say, "I think it'd be more productive to think about ways to figure this out together, as opposed to bemoan the fact that we don't have what we once had and what we have become." Jim Nicola responded that he didn't think those raising the past had been bemoaning as much as trying to make sure they had the history. Frost agreed but said (drawing a brief silence from the room in response), "the reality is we need each other to do *anything*—to do *anything* now." The increasing interdependency (or perhaps codependency) of the two sectors, while never stated in such terms explicitly, would also emerge as a key topic the next day.

Jim Nicola added that, from his vantage point, "audiences are wearing out on the little small play, in the living room, with a sofa" or "the solo piece" and that one of the bigger issues in the sector is the lack of resources for large-scale *plays* (as opposed to musicals), which the commercial world is generally not interested in supporting. He characterized these large-scale plays as "a version of a big thing that needs to be fed."

Commercial producer Kevin McCollum suggested that if nonprofit theaters wanted to have the ongoing resources to sustain artists then they needed to start thinking about owning copyrights. He then resurrected the drug metaphor, this time taking it in a new direction. The analogy McCollum seemed to make was that theaters (like drug companies) are research and development enterprises that produce experiences that have a powerful effect on audiences (drugs) and that (like drug companies with patents) theaters need to own and exploit intellectual property and then reinvest profits back into creating more work (new drugs).

> They develop a drug—"the hair on the back of your neck stands up." Let's call this the drug we created for theater. You do that five times and you've got a hit new work. Then you're in the position of distributing that drug around the world, and you get a little piece of that. And scientists who developed that with you get to keep the majority of the patent, perhaps. … We're a research and development business. We're structured like manufacturing. The whole economic stream from commercial to noncommercial is messed up. If we think of ourselves as a drug company, we will find the right economic structure.

David Dower, associate artistic director at Arena Stage and moderator for the convening, remarked, "So we're not the *consumers* of the drugs, we're the *manufacturers* of them," eliciting a good deal of laughter from the room.

Reflecting further on the need for a new business model, Gregory Mosher suggested at one point that perhaps both the commercial and nonprofit forms had become a bit of a trap and that it might be useful to look at new models like the Low-Profit Limited Liability Corporation (L3C).[13]

A bit later, picking up on Breglio's "too big to fail" description of some of the largest theater institutions, I asked Rocco Landesman whether, if (indeed) some organizations had become too big to take the risks that they were created to take and were increasingly dependent on commercial programming and income to survive, it then stood to reason that some new quasi-commercial tax status category was needed (with fewer tax benefits to theaters but greater freedom), or perhaps some type of regulation of the sector?

Landesman began by saying, first and foremost, from the standpoint of the NEA, the sector needed vastly more resources at all levels—and certainly more than "the NEA with its current budget constraints could ever provide." He relayed that The Public Theater, with its "$20-something million budget," receives $60,000 from the NEA and then noted in jest that he was surprised Oskar Eustis even returned his phone calls. (Eustis was quick to say that The Public appreciated its $60,000 grant.) Landesman stated that the NEA was endeavoring to support work of the highest excellence that was *also* venturesome and risk taking. The implication of his comments seemed to be that, rather than revising the tax code, perhaps funders could influence the

---

[13]According to the definition on Wikipedia, a low-profit limited liability company (L3C) is a legal form of business entity in the United States that was created to bridge the gap between nonprofit and for-profit investing by providing a structure that facilitates investments in socially beneficial, for-profit ventures while simplifying compliance with IRS rules for Program Related Investments.

arts sector by directing funds (to the best of their ability) to those best supporting nonprofit ideals.

I then raised John Breglio's earlier comment that the resident theater movement's ideals were being upheld, in many cases, by smaller theaters but noted that these smaller theaters didn't appear to be a priority for many foundations or the NEA. Landesman replied that the NEA was trying to prioritize such theaters. I returned to the question of tax status and asked Landesman whether it seemed possible that some theaters had become "commercial theaters in disguise" and, if so, whether something should be done about this?

While not answered directly by Landesman, the question was met with a chorus of yeses and nos from across the room. Mosher again suggested that perhaps shifting to a different tax status (L3C, for example) could provide theaters with the possibility of working with commercial investors without putting their tax status at risk, and advised that since there wouldn't be more money coming from the government in the next ten years, it might be time to consider such alternatives.

But a rather loud, dissenting voice in the crowd was that of Jim Nicola of New York Theatre Workshop. Nicola responded: "That's off track. Why do you want to take a tax break away from people that are trying?" He said that he was also concerned about the message that "big is bad and small is good" or that "institutions are bad." Mara Isaacs of McCarter Theatre added that because a relatively small number of organizations outside of New York were actually getting enhancement money, getting into the "tax codes and nonprofit models" was "a little bit of a red herring." She reiterated that she felt the group was looking at the wrong problem.

Perhaps We Still Haven't Found the Right Problem?

Towards the end of the session, Rocco Landesman asked the room, "So what's the right problem?" to which Gregory Mosher responded that from his perspective, one "big problem is that a playwright works on a play for two years and gets $7,500." Landesman picked up on the topic of artists wages—one that he has raised on numerous occasions, including at the January 2011 convening "From Scarcity to Abundance" at Arena Stage—and questioned the economic structure of the theater industry given how difficult it was for theater artists to make "a decent or credible or any kind of dignified living working in the field."

Before bringing the first session to a close, I offered Mosher and Landesman the opportunity to offer any final thoughts. Mosher remarked that he had grown to hate the phrases "right to fail" or "freedom to fail" as he feared that they would start to cover the "freedom to phone it in." Mosher then shared an anecdote from his time at LCT aimed at conveying how he and Bernard Gersten had tried to create circumstances where artists could do their best work.

> I said to the director, "How long do you want to rehearse?" and he would invariably say, "Well, how long do I have?" And I would say, "You have as long as you want." And there was a long pause and he would say, "No, really, how long do I have?" And they almost always said five weeks, plus tech, plus three weeks of previews; but then Mbongeni Ngema said "A year." So I said, "Great!" And we rehearsed *Sarafina!* for a year. That made a huge difference. And the ten dollar—never forget that the *ten dollar tickets* are what primed Lincoln Center. ... And we held to that ten dollars through seven years. And that made a difference. So that's one thought: how do you create circumstances where people can do their best work?

Landesman (who had attended the two previous meetings in 1974 and 2000), then offered a general commentary on the tenor of the meeting thus far, noting "to have a conversation this interesting and this stimulating among people who agree is very unusual. It's noteworthy. We'll see how it evolves." To which David Dower quipped, "Yeah. No chairs thrown yet." Landesman then remarked on the chaos of 1974, describing it as "complete madness," "a zoo," "wild," and "highly contentious."

While the first session ended with no consensus on the "right problem," as the conversation continued there would be a growing agreement that a major problem in the nonprofit theater sector—if not the only one—might very well be one of lost values.

The session ended with Bob Brustein sharing an anecdote:

> Our first year at Yale, we did a *Prometheus Bound* directed by Jonathan Miller. And David Merrick came up to see it. I don't know why he did. And after he saw it he went out saying, "The name of the game is still entertainment."

Everyone chuckled as they headed to a coffee break.

HOW WE GOT HERE: ROBERT BRUSTEIN

In conversation with Oskar Eustis

First, we must take our gaze and any preoccupation away, away from Broadway, from which we took our leave many years ago. If they want what we discover, nourish and perform, that's okay, though if we have acting companies, we will lose them. But Broadway must not invade our house and take over our home. Always: he who pays the piper calls the tune.—Zelda Fichandler

The second panel was originally intended to be a discussion between Zelda Fichandler, founder of Arena Stage, and Bob Brustein, moderated by Oskar Eustis, on the topic of the formation of the resident theater movement and its evolution. While Zelda Fichandler was, regrettably, unable to participate in the event at Arena Stage due to family obligations, she was able to lend her voice to the conversation. Eustis brought to the meeting a copy of the keynote address that Fichandler had delivered at a Stage Directors and Choreographers Society event in Washington, DC, just a few nights prior and referred to it several times throughout the discussion.[14] He started

---

[14]Fichandler's talk was given at the annual awards ceremony of the Stage Directors and Choreographers Society, at which the third annual Zelda Fichandler Award was presented to the artistic director of The Wilma Theater, Blanka Ziska. http://www.howlround.com/zelda-fichandler-address-to-the-stage-directors-and-choreographers-society-in-celebration-of-the-third-annual-zelda-fichandler-award-delivered-october-26-2011/

the session by suggesting that it might be useful to discuss why this entity, the nonprofit theater, was created in the first place given that there was a "thriving commercial theater in this country, before what we call nonprofit theater was formed."

Eustis first read extensively from Fichandler's keynote and then asked Brustein to "reflect on Zelda's words." Eustis, quoting Fichandler:

> What drew us to the way we went? What was the vision, the inciting incident? Actually, there was no incident, no high drama, there was simply a change of thought, a new way of looking at things, a tilt of the head, a revolution in our perception. We looked at what we had—the hit-or-miss; put-it-up, tear-it-down; make-a-buck, lose-a-buck; discontinuous; artist-indifferent; New York-centered ways of Broadway, and they weren't tolerable anymore, and it made us angry. We thought there had to be a better way, and we made that up out of what was lying around ungathered and, standing on the shoulders of earlier efforts in America and examples common in other countries, we went forward, some of us starting small, some like the Guthrie, big.
>
> The fabric of the thought that propelled us was that theatre should stop serving the function of making money, for which it has never been and never will be suited, and start serving the revelation and shaping of the process of living, for which it is uniquely suited, for which it, indeed, exists. The new thought was that theatre should be restored to itself as a form of art. Perhaps we should simply call ourselves art theatres. What do you think?
>
> There's an expressive word, I believe it's Sanskrit—and the word is apava that translates as "the effective means to make a vision concrete" or workable or real. Our apava, strangely enough, turned out to be the nonprofit corporation. Some of us might take that fact for granted, but we shouldn't. It's the basic reality of our existence. Before nineteen hundred and fifty something, theatre was excluded from the benefits given to science, universities, charities, the church, opera, and maybe

dance—but not theatre, because it made a profit. We knew that without the nonprofit blanket we could not exist, for it allows us to receive gifts and grants and to be free of taxes on tickets.

Precursors to a Movement: Small, Poor Art Theaters and Decentralized Federal Theaters

When prompted to reflect on Fichandler's words, Bob Brustein began by reminding the room that there was, of course, a precedent for the resident theater movement, the Federal Theatre, and that before the Federal Theatre there were "art theaters" (Provincetown Playhouse, Cherry Lane, and others) but that they "didn't have subsidies." He continued:

> They might have had some angel in the wings, but there was no structure really for year-by-year support of them and they had to depend on the box office. And there wasn't much. Their annual budget was about four-and-a-half dollars.

Brustein then walked the room through the short but impactful life of the Federal Theatre Project (FTP), a manifestation of the Works Progress Administration (WPA), which was a depression-era New Deal program created under the presidency of Franklin Delano Roosevelt to stimulate the economy and raise employment. As Brustein put it, "Roosevelt had the good sense to recognize that among the unemployed were not only steel workers and automobile workers but people in the arts."

Hallie Flanagan, who had been a professor at Vassar, was put in charge of the program. Brustein characterized her as a "brilliant choice" and remarked, "Before long she had created about 400 theaters in this country." He noted that, whereas before the American theater was entirely "focused around Broadway and then touring out of Broadway," the FTP was "decentralized. It was multicultural. There were black groups, there were Latino groups; there were classical groups. There were all forms of theater being produced at this time, and she was encouraging them."

After four short years, the Federal Theatre was shut down, Brustein relayed, "because the House on Un-American Activities Committee decided it was communist." Following the collapse of the FTP, Brustein explained, came the nine-year period of The Group Theatre, "led by a very passionate idealist named Harold Clurman." Brustein conveyed that The Group Theatre couldn't survive, because, as Clurman himself had remarked, The Group was "operating as an art theater under a profit formula." Brustein then recounted the evolution from The Group Theatre to The Actors Studio and then turned to the subject of Lincoln Center Theater, which was formed around this same time (in 1965).

He described LCT as "a nonprofit theater, unfortunately run by people who had nothing but profit experience: Elia Kazan and Robert Whitehead, with Bobby Lewis doing the teaching." Brustein lamented that the American theater was "moving away from the idealism of the Federal Theatre and the Group Theatre into a more commercial venue"—a shift, he suggested, that one could see manifested "in the first season of Lincoln Center."

The Resident Theater Movement: A World of Values Separate from Profit and Commerce

Bob Brustein described this arc in the American theater as "a gradual thinning of ambitions" and said that it was out of this environment that the resident theater movement was created. He held up as one of the great examples Sir Tyrone Guthrie, one of the pioneers of the movement like Zelda Fichandler, who "went around to a number of cities trying to find a place to put his theater." Brustein noted the "interesting" fact that before accepting the offer to come to Minneapolis, Guthrie "turned down Boston because it was too close to New York."

Brustein mentioned a few of the early theaters and then broke off saying that he wouldn't run through the entire list. Eustis added that Brustein himself had started two theaters, one in New Haven (Yale Repertory Theatre) and the other in Cambridge (American Repertory Theater), and then asked Brustein, "So what were you trying to do? I mean, why not do commercial theater? What is it that you were trying to accomplish that was different?"

Brustein responded by recounting a few highlights from his extraordinary theater career. Brustein dropped out of Yale Drama School after one year and started a theater called Studio Seven at the Provincetown Playhouse (O'Neill's old theater) with a number of other students from Yale (called the Odets group because they had spent a year rehearsing a production of *Awake and Sing!*). He then joined a resident classical repertory company, Theater on the Green at Wellesley (originally called Group Twenty), which he recalled as "one of the most exciting and delightful experiences of my life, because I was working with people I loved on projects that I loved and we all had a common viewpoint." He was eventually called by Kingman Brewster to become Dean of the School of Drama at Yale, where he got the idea to develop a resident theater aligned with a drama school. He worked for thirteen years to develop a rotating repertory system at Yale before transitioning to Harvard (with his acting company from Yale) where he founded the American Repertory Theater.

Reflecting on these snapshots from Brustein's career, Oskar Eustis remarked:

> What strikes me as you talk, Bob, is that ... everything you're talking about is about being part of a larger history that stems back really to that beach in Provincetown in 1920 through to the present. And you talk about being engaged in the training and the discussion and the creation all at once so that, in a way, you are creating a world of values that is separate. And that world of values is part of a larger history; but we haven't talked about profit or commerce in any of this really. And I think that one of the difficult things is: Where do you find an alternative set of values in the world—where you can live inside an alternative set of conversations to the conversations about "profit and loss"?

Brustein responded that he "was lucky enough to start this theater, or these theaters, at a time when they were really fashionable. And there was support coming from the foundations." Eustis continued:

IN THE INTERSECTION

> The thing that has been certainly inspiring to me about your life and career, Bob, is that there's a sense that you've created a web of a story that's bigger than ... just individual shows and bigger than just the individual institutions (Yale Rep and ART). ... By my being able to claim you as a forebear, I'm existing within a lineage that gives me a sense of belonging to a tribe—so it's a family. That is just crucial for my happiness within the nonprofit field. ... I'm trying to keep strong a sense of an alternative perspective.

Brustein countered, "We went through a lot of hell at Yale." He noted rebellions, revolts, student uprisings, a threat from the SDS to shut down his theater during a production of *Don Juan*, and directives to stop teaching on any subject except the Black Panthers. Capping off a description of this tumultuous period in which people were "interested in everything but the arts" (unless they were "highly inflammatory and devoted towards changing things"), he said:

> So my wife gets a call one night and the caller says, "Is Brustein there?" And she says, "No." And he says, "Tell the pig he's going to die." ... And actually a bullet was shot through the window of my neighbor, Richard Elman, and I thought, "that shot was meant for me."

Eustis then brought Zelda Fichandler back into the conversation, reading:

> First, we must take our gaze and any preoccupation away, away from Broadway, from which we took our leave many years ago. If they want what we discover, nourish, and perform, that's OK, though if we have acting companies, we will lose them. But Broadway must not invade our house and take over our home. Always: he who pays the piper calls the tune.
>
> Next, a theatre institution, in and of itself, is an artwork, a collaborative artwork whose principal artist is the artistic director. The artwork is not truly alive until it meets its audience, so that we

absolutely want and must have the audience with us, responding with their imagination and belief. But it is we who choose and create the work. Neither Picasso nor Beethoven asked anyone what they wanted to see or hear. That comes from deep within each individual artist. The artist may be lonely or feel unsure of, or inadequate to, what she is making, but she must cling to her integrity—her wholeness—and see it through. Being an artistic director, like growing old, is not for sissies. And smaller theatres are easier.

… The audience comes into the theatre with today's newspaper under its arm, and popular culture in its eyes and ears. The artistic director has to live straddling two realities: the unique imaginary world of the play; the other, the real world beyond the doors and who is living there, within range of the theatre's voice. All theatre is political—the Latin polis, of and about the people. And the artistic director has to read her texts with that in mind and construct her seasons accordingly.

… I'm omitting a consideration of our financial problems, though I ponder them all the time. Especially the price of tickets, which is a form of censorship, saying who comes in and who stays out. The Royal Shakespeare Company's New York five-play series sold out at $250 a ticket with a $50 surcharge—$1,500 for the series. None of my friends were able to go. In our own theatres, do we really want to imitate USAir and raise prices incrementally as seats get scarcer? Do we absolutely have to do this for survival's sake?

Brustein remarked, "She's a real visionary human being. The true grandmother of this movement and a very good writer."

Distinctions in the Intersection: Of Purpose, Money, Deals, and Programming

Before opening up the conversation to the room, Bob Brustein said that he wanted to say something about commercial production:

I've obviously been a big enemy of that. But I'm an enemy of the *frequency* of it. I think it's inevitable from time to time. The question is keeping some sort of a constraint on it. Whether you want to or not, one of those shows is going to go.

The last comment (said rather earnestly) made several people laugh. Christopher Ashley, artistic director of the nonprofit La Jolla Playhouse, made the case that the intersection between commercial and nonprofit, proportionally, represents a "pretty small part" of what the theater does and that the "commercial problem exists largely in musicals," because while most nonprofits can produce plays on their own, very few could commission, create, develop, and produce a musical without help and some kind of subsidy. Moreover, he said it is important to keep in perspective that all of the nonprofit institutions in the room "have very vibrant education programs, are commissioning artists, are doing readings and workshops of new work—have all kinds of stuff that does not touch the commercial realm."

Of his own experience stepping into the intersection (rather unwittingly it would later be revealed), Brustein told the story of Rocco Landesman bringing him a script by a mutual friend and former student, Bill Hauptman, an adaptation of *Huckleberry Finn* that would eventually go on to become the tremendously successful Broadway musical, *Big River*. Like *A Chorus Line* and *Rent*, *Big River* also represented a watershed moment for the field because it is one of the earliest instances of a commercial producer successfully developing (and enhancing) a production at a nonprofit resident theater before moving it to Broadway. Brustein did the first production at American Repertory Theater (ART). It was cast almost entirely with ART company members and directed by Des McAnuff. Following the first production, changes were made and it was then produced at McAnuff's theater, the La Jolla Playhouse. Following the La Jolla run, it was determined that, with some changes, the show was ready to move to Broadway. Commenting on this trajectory Brustein said:

> And we were happy to see it on Broadway, happy to see it get a larger audience. It was an extraordinary production. But we were also happy that we had no part in the producing of it [on

Broadway] and I thought that was important. We were happy to get our, whatever it was, three percent, four percent.

Michael David, Landesman's partner at Dodger Theatricals, jumped in to say that he and Landesman had done a few other deals with nonprofits and that "to Bob's credit" he "wouldn't take any money, in terms of enhancement, which didn't have a name at the time." While Brustein's comments suggested that he was fine with a theater taking royalties, he expressed concerns about enhancement money and cautioned the room, "we have to beware of it and keep our eye on it."

Ashley suggested that, for the purposes of the two-day conversation, it would be useful to distinguish between *enhancement* money ("the money that you take to make the play happen at your theater") and *royalties* ("the passive income that you later get from a show as it moves on"), and acknowledge that they effect organizations differently. Ashley also reiterated a point made by Oskar Eustis and others earlier: like *A Chorus Line* for The Public and *Rent* for New York Theatre Workshop, royalty income from *Jersey Boys* had made it possible for "a whole community of people to earn their money" and had enabled La Jolla Playhouse to pay salaries and commissions to artists and keep its set and costume shops running.

Commercial producer Kevin McCollum seconded Ashley's point that most of the work happening in the intersection is around musicals, but added two additional explanations for the activity, beyond the need for subsidy for nonprofits striving to produce musicals: nonprofits generally don't have the *rights* (which often sit with commercial producers) and commercial producers are often seeking out nonprofits because they need an *audience* to "take [the work] to the next level."

McCollum then made the point that these deals come about two different ways. He contrasted the *Big River* scenario of the commercial producer approaching the nonprofit to get an audience with a different (but increasingly frequent) scenario of a nonprofit theater developing a project for several years and soliciting the commercial producer for participation. In this second scenario, he said, the nonprofit wants to find a partner it can trust, with equal passion, because it has to go on and produce six more shows that season. He summed up, "You're talking about the money, but the sinewy material that keeps us all coming to this frustrating and glorious industry is we're passion junkies."

Brustein would then speak from his "long history" and point out that "something important is different today than it was, say, fifty years ago, sixty years go." He mentioned that his first teaching job was at Cornell, where he was paid $3,600 per year, and his second was at Vassar, where he was paid $4,200 per year. He then continued:

> We didn't expect to make hundreds of thousands of dollars. And there was no raiding going on from one university to another to get a star and offer to pay a certain amount. That's what's happening now. Now you have the star of Berkeley who is raided by Harvard and offered $100,000 more than he's [currently] making. This is a complete distortion of what the original aims of academic scholarship were about.
>
> And I think the same thing is happening to us in the profit and nonprofit theater. There was a separation between the two. There's a separation between serious literature and popular literature. The same critics do not cover the same kinds of books. ... There are differences then and they are dying. They are being impaired. They are folding into each other.

Kevin McCollum picked up on the "popular" versus "serious" distinction saying, "There's a joke that says the more important the play, the less people have seen it." Responding to Brustein's comments he questioned the usefulness of separating the two things:

> I believe the best thing is when something that's expected to be serious or important becomes popular. ... Even though art is a way to reflect chaos, I believe very strongly that the separation

of what's important or what's popular, or serious and popular, should be blurred. ... What I don't think you realize is that the blurring is your way out. The blurring is the ability to say it is important and it is popular. And that's what creates greatness.

Brustein replied, "You don't know what's going to be popular" (to which McCollum agreed) and then shared the story of *'night Mother* by Marsha Norman, which had been rejected by forty theaters because of its difficult subject matter (suicide). Brustein produced the play, which went on to become one of the most popular plays the theater ever produced. He made a similar point about Milan Kundera's "very abstruse play," *Jacques and his Master*—also rather "abstrusely directed" by Susan Sontag—which had people "flocking from all over the city" to the theater.

He Who Pays the Piper Calls the Tune

With the preamble, "you have to keep listening to these people, Zelda [Fichandler] and Bob [Brustein]; it's the only thing to have faith in ..." former lawyer and current producer John Breglio picked up on the proverb used by Zelda Fichandler, "He who pays the piper calls the tune" and reflected on the influence of various sources of income in the nonprofit sector over time.

(Though Breglio and others sometimes used the word *piper*, it seemed clear that what they were actually referring to were *those paying the pipers to play*):

> If you go back to the very beginning of what Bob [Brustein] was talking about [the Federal Theatre Project] and whoever paid the piper back then ... no one was really telling those people what to do. They were doing what they wanted to do.... It was pure. That was a pure moment in time.
>
> We then went from *that* to the not-for-profit structure, the IRS code, and that was what made it possible for people to create the beginnings of the regional system and all the great theaters

that Bob mentioned. The piper there is really the taxpayer, OK, because you're getting a tax exempt status. The taxpayer is paying for that. The government is paying for that. But the piper there is so *amorphous*. ... And then we had a great period of time when you have philanthropy and corporations and foundations who were giving great support; and even the government was giving more money—New York State Council for the Arts. So the piper there ... just wanted to make sure you were still pure to your mission.

Unfortunately, the piper [payer] now, which is the only one left, is the commercial theater. ... There was a turning point when the AIDS crisis hit and after 9/11. We saw a huge drop off for the arts in terms of philanthropy from foundations and corporations because, quite frankly, we were not a priority. ... We lost huge amounts of money and we have never recovered that, ever. I'm saying, with that vacuum, what has happened is that vacuum was filled by commercial producers coming in.

In the midst of Breglio's description, NYTW's Jim Nicola interjected to say that foundations, governments, and individuals also give money with conditions attached to it—a subject to which he would return. Breglio reiterated his point that money coming from commercial producers had a different impact:

... I'm just saying that when that piper is sitting across from you, as a not-for-profit ... it is very, very difficult when you're taking that money to keep in mind what your status is, what your not-for-profit purpose is, what your mission is, what drives you to do what you should be doing. And that tension is, I think, everything we're talking about. And I'm not making a qualitative judgment. You have to address it. That's the reality.

Producer Michael David spoke up and challenged two of Breglio's suggestions: (1) that "cigar chewing" commercial producers and nonprofit producers "with steady salaries and 401(k)s" (as David characterized them), were working together primarily because of a subsidy vacuum that had been created; and (2) that the money from commercial producers made it difficult for nonprofits to stay true to their missions and values. David continued:

> Since 1984 we've created two dozen relationships with artistic directors and theaters, seminal theaters as Bob [Brustein] called them. Here's the naïve part: our relationships began because we thought we could share our enthusiasm for a particular project with someone else who happened to have a job in a seminal theater. And with that shared enthusiasm we would then talk about what we could do together to put it up. And the budget conversation happened afterward. It's a dance, you know. ... What I'm suggesting is that, this may be naïve, that I never really thought when we went to someone and said, "*Into the Woods* is really good" that what they saw was a dollar sign when we walked in.
>
> The fact is *we have good ideas too*! And so we found people that wanted to share those good ideas; and the fact that we were from different institutions or different places, became incidental. Now, I couldn't be more afraid of what's happening out there. I'm a passionate theater person more than anything else and I look to the nonprofit to do the things we can't possibly dare to do in that stupid place we work. But please don't minimize our passion, insight, perhaps even taste, by suggesting that if we happen to bring it to you there's got to be something wrong with it.

Oskar Eustis replied that he "would never minimize that" and that a couple of the smartest people he knew working in the American theater, "people with fantastic taste," worked exclusively in the commercial sector.

Crossing a Line: Losing Artistic Control

Responding to Kevin McCollum's description of the two ways in which commercial nonprofit partnerships arise, Oskar Eustis admitted that the scenario in which a commercial producer brings a project to a nonprofit (the *Big River* model) felt like "a line" for him, "a threshold" he would not cross. He asked if others felt the same way. McCollum interjected to make the point that nonprofit and commercial producers were trying to do the same thing—that they were "trying to make great work." But La Jolla's Christopher Ashley picked up on Eustis's question, acknowledging that there was another danger when crossing the line—beyond the slippery slope of how to define success—and that was "loss of control."

Related to this topic, Ashley had commented earlier in the session on a "fundamental difference" between the nonprofit and commercial realms: commercial works are *projects* for which producers are trying to develop the largest audience—what he characterized as "one-offs"—whereas nonprofits are in a "community of artists and audiences" and engaged in a "much longer term conversation." Ashley reminded the group that Michael Ritchie at Center Theatre Group had to cancel his plans to attend the meeting at Arena Stage because, as had been widely reported in the news, a production of *Funny Girl* that had been slated to open at his theater in a matter of weeks had fallen out of his season because the commercial producer had been unable to fully capitalize it. Ashley made the point, "One of the downsides to that partnership is that whatever promise you've made to your audience as a theater is not completely within your control anymore. And that's real."

Providing a possible reason for the failure of *Funny Girl* to capitalize, Kevin McCollum made the point that, increasingly, in order to get commitments from stars and investors for the nonprofit production, the commercial producer must be able to guarantee a Broadway transfer (that is, secure a Broadway theater and raise the much larger sum needed to capitalize the Broadway production).

Later in the discussion, echoing Ashley's comments about loss of control, Eustis explained why he's never taken a show that's been brought to him by a commercial producer saying:

> Actually, my feeling when I run institutions is that I've been
> invested with a great charge, which is the husbandry and

stewardship of an institution that is fundamentally belonging to the community. It belongs to everybody. That's why it has a 501(c)(3). It has a 501(c)(3) because nobody but the people own it. And theoretically, what my job is, is to *defend* that mission, to *align* with that mission. ... But I realize why I've never crossed that line. I can't imagine putting a show on in one of my theaters that I'm not responsible for the artistic choices.

Kevin McCollum responded. He first asked commercial producer Michael David how many projects he had in development at the time (David said eight). McCollum then noted how many he had in development and described why these partnerships are necessary from the commercial producer's perspective to carry the projects forward, and why they need not result in less artistic participation from the nonprofit:

I have seven. That means I've already done the research on the project, I've acquired the rights, we're planning workshops, and at some point we're saying, "Now we need to add an audience." We're not going to open cold on Broadway. We're not even going to open cold with a musical Off-Broadway. Because the economics, we know, is a real estate game. So what do you do? Well, there's all these wonderful, glorious institutions supported by communities—with great dramaturgs, great artistic directors. And we might have already chosen the director; but then it becomes a dialogue. Well, what designers do you work with, or have worked with, and do you like? And then it becomes a partnership.

I never take a show that's fully done. I get a couple of songs and people that want to work together. I start taking them to lunch. Taking them to the back room and working through what the story could be. Because I don't have to report to a board of directors. I don't have to do any of that. I've done that already and I felt slowed down by it.

IN THE INTERSECTION

McCollum asked Eustis why he assumed a writer brought to him by a commercial producer would not be one he would want to work with and then suggested, "Imagine me as one of your directors of [play] development coming to you and saying, 'Hey, we discovered this!' The fact that I don't work for you doesn't mean you're not going to have just as much collaborative input." But Eustis was not buying the analogy of commercial producer (with rights to the project, money invested, and a director attached) as "director of play development" and noted that the two things were "completely different."

McCollum then outlined a scenario in which he could collaborate with The Public to produce the work with no money being transferred to The Public. But Eustis's response suggested that taking money was not the problem. Bob Brustein then joined the conversation, which began to home in on the issue of artistic control.

B. Brustein: But why should he take the show?

K. McCollum: He shouldn't take it if he doesn't like it; but what if he does?

B. Brustein: It's not a matter of liking it or not. Does it fit into his institution?

[overlapping dialogue from others]

O. Eustis: Here's the thing [*quoting from Zelda Fichandler's speech*], "a theatre institution, in and of itself, is an artwork, a collaborative artwork whose principal artist is the artistic director." My question is not whether I like it or not. My question is … I have to be able to look everybody, including my board of directors, including my audience, in the eye, and say, "I'm responsible for what's there on stage." And that means if I can't hire and fire the director, if I can't cast the show—

Unidentifiable Voice: You would be able to hire and fire the director.

M. David: This is about *process* too.

There's More Than One Way to Compromise the Process

Tony Taccone (artistic director at Berkeley Repertory Theatre) then joined the conversation and suggested that partnerships with commercial producers were not the only way to "rob your theater of its own investment." He was referring to co-productions with other nonprofits.

> T. Taccone: We share shows now: co-pro. Of the ten shows that Berkeley Rep is doing this year, every single one is shared. You talk about an economic model. *That's* an economic model.

> B. Brustein: It's called McTheater.

> O. Eustis: No, not necessarily.

Taccone then elaborated on ways that process and mission are compromised by such co-productions and spoke about the need to address this issue:

> The problem for us with shared shows is frequently that there is a lack of commitment on the deepest possible level on the part of the staff when we receive a show. The audience doesn't care; [it] wants to see good shows. But every other single aspect of the organization that touches that show is less engaged than when we make something.
>
> We were charged with making things. With making things from our own sensibilities, from our own politics, from our own desires. And when we shortchange that? We've had to figure out ways to survive and by doing so, in large part, we tend to shortchange that process. And that process is why we do it. And if you can't find ways to redouble and reenergize yourself with the process, you're kind of fucking yourself. And we've been doing that incrementally, slowly, for all the right reasons. And I find there [are] really a lot of well-intentioned, smart people who

are courageous and still committed to doing work that has value, that is engaged in the world, and that wants to change things. But the way that we are disconnected somehow from the product, and the pressure to make more product, has had an effect.

And I think I'm here to figure that out. How do I regenerate my institution and myself so that I can survive? Because it ain't going away! Hyper-capitalism is not going away—at least in my lifetime. But there's got to be a different way to think about the work and to reinvest in the making of it so that it touches as many people in my organization as possible. Because that is the way to actually move great shows: make great work in your own theater.

Echoing sentiments by Oskar Eustis and Taccone, but from the other side of the table, David Binder explained why he, as a commercial producer, never worked in a *nonprofit* context:

D. Binder: I want to *make* the thing. I don't want to give it to [a nonprofit] to make. Otherwise, what am I doing?"

M. David: You're *developing* it. And you're giving it one step.

At this point John Breglio was hankering to say something; however, his comments would need to wait until the next session on contracts, which he was leading with Michael David. David closed the session commenting, "I do think *how* this relationship works makes it good or terrible. And, indeed, that *process* is part of, perhaps, the solution."

EVOLUTION OF THE INTERSECTION: CONTRACTS
John Breglio and Michael David

Moderated by David Dower

> We're all afraid of legalities. And they get in
> the way of practical collaboration.—Kevin McCollum

> But it's more than a legal issue. It goes to the heart
> of what a not-for-profit organization is.—John Breglio

The third panel began with a chart being distributed that showed a breakdown of the elements covered in the contracts governing the developmental collaborations between Dodger Theatricals and various nonprofit theaters from 1984 through 2010. (Dodger Theatricals is a commercial producing company that was founded by Michael David and Rocco Landesman with Des McAnuff and Edward Strong.) David Dower began the session by asking Michael David to walk people through the document.[15] Michael David got a chuckle when he began by saying that he and his partners had created this chart some time ago as they imagined that TCG was already tracking all the deals "made between the enemy and the seminal theaters."

---

[15] To avoid confusion, throughout this section of the report, David Dower is referenced by his last name (Dower) and Michael David is referenced using his full name.

While it was never stated explicitly at the meeting whether any individual nonprofits or collectives of organizations (through LORT or TCG, for instance) had ever compiled a document charting the evolution of the contracts made with commercial producers, one sensed from the curiosity about the document when it was distributed that it represented new information for the group.

The Contract vs. The Dance

The first point Michael David made was that the chart was comprised almost exclusively of new work (only two classics) and that, with the exception of two shows, none of them had a destination at the time that they were produced at the nonprofits. He described it as "a purchase—an investment in wisdom gathering. That's it." David Dower asked whether "nothing had a destination" meant the project didn't yet have a theater in New York. Michael David responded, "Right. We weren't saying, 'We've got to be on Broadway in eight weeks.'" He then added, "And we weren't doing it because the scenery was cheaper if we did it with someone else, or whatever. This was *research* and *development*." Michael David then described the laissez faire nature of the process used by Dodger Theatricals saying:

> We go through the early dance of creating a contract like this. ...
> We sign the paper. We get out of the way. We have no control over what's going on whatsoever. We come to the opening night. We don't want our name on it. None of it. And it's been that way for twenty-something years. ... No *ménage à trois* ... no different intentions trying to cross over.
> "We've got a date to make and it's got to be fixed"—*that's* the great adulterator and it seems to me it's what poisons these relationships.

Oskar Eustis then asked Michael David to say more about selection of creative personnel. Michael David responded after a pause, "It's the dance." He then described the dance:

> People will agree or they won't. ... We're attempting to find someone like-minded for something that we're doing with Moisés Kauffman. Now, we'll look for someone who's worked on other Moisés works before and say, "If you like Moisés would you be interested in this sort of thing?" They might agree. But we don't *cast* it.

A bit later in the conversation, Rocco Landesman, Michael David's former partner, offered a slightly different perspective on the casting process saying, "Mike, you can't say there was never any conversation about who's going to play certain roles." Michael David countered that those discussions happened "at the beginning" of the process. He elaborated:

> You might say, "We'd like to sit in on casting of the four principals" and someone would say "no" or "yes." And depending on whether you're willing to, sort of, learn from what you might think is the hobbled cast (because you're not there), you either do or you don't—because you can always walk away from this.

The distinction between things agreed to before signing the contract versus after would prove to be an important one as the two-day discussion continued.

Dower then asked for clarification on whether a row of the chart marked *Artistic Team* was the area that covered the selection of creative personnel. Michael David confirmed that it was. In all cases but two (in which the selection rested with the nonprofit) this relationship was described as *mutual*. When asked later to clarify one of the two productions where the artistic team was assembled by the nonprofit, Michael David said it was "one of the things we don't like to do." In this instance a nonprofit had brought a project to Dodger Theatricals after the production was put together (and already cast) and the nonprofit was simply seeking a financial investment. He commented, "It was sort of a boring relationship where they got the fun of doing it all. It was ready to go someplace else and we were, um, unworthy pack horses."

Echoing Kevin McCollum's earlier comment about rights to musicals often resting with commercial producers, Michael David then clarified another row of the chart, *Term of License*, saying "in almost all of these we've had those licenses, so either we give permission for the author to give a limited license to the seminal theater, or we give a limited license to the theater." Over the course of the two days there would be several references to nonprofits entering into partnerships with commercial producers because the commercial producers owned the rights to a work the nonprofit wanted to produce.

John Breglio then returned to the issue of "mutual" decisions with regard to the artistic team, and asked Michael David to clarify whether these were "mutual decisions between you and the not-for-profit at the very beginning" and, if so, whether, in the case of a dispute, the not-for-profit could, for example, fire the director. Michael David confirmed Breglio's interpretation saying, "Absolutely. We have no control."

Commercial producer David Binder probed this point a bit asking, rather incredulously, "So you guys are in previews, and the show is in La Jolla, or what not, and you guys, literally, *you don't give a note*?" Michael David responded, "No" and then elaborated on the topic.

Tiptoeing Around the Legalities

Michael David's response suggested that the hands-off approach of Dodger Theatricals was motivated by perceived legal constraints:

> It was the *rule*. And our rule. I mean, we may be there looking at everything we possibly can ... But beyond that: no. That's the *rule*.

Michael David then suggested that commercial producers were not *there* to get in the way of nonprofits, rather to learn from them, and that such an approach is what keeps the peace. John Breglio then stepped in to clarify the legal situation:

> J. Breglio: If the contract says they're in control, there's no harm you
> showing up at previews and having a drink with the artistic director
> and talking about what you think about the show. I mean, it's wonderful
> that you've expressed your hands-off attitude; but I'm just making a
> distinction about what you could do without any prohibition against it.
>
> M. David: No, we're not uncollegial. … All we're saying is
> basically that, in the end, the nonprofit doesn't have to, if they
> don't want to, talk to you before they do something.

It would later emerge in the course of the conversation, however, that a majority of contracts between commercial producers and nonprofits (including those used by Dodger Theatricals) state something to the contrary: that the nonprofit must, under certain circumstances, get permission from the commercial producer before taking certain actions (for instance, firing a member of the creative team or extending the run of a show). The discussion around artistic control would turn out to be one of the more important and complex over the course of the two days.

David Dower next asked for clarification on the row marked *Control* noting that in every instance shown on the chart, control rested with the nonprofit. He inquired, "What would be the opposite of that?" The conversation that ensued, largely between the two attorneys in the room (John Breglio and Loren Plotkin), highlights some of the difficulties commercial producers, nonprofits, and the lawyers that represent them face when endeavoring to collaborate *legally*.

> D. Dower: Has anybody had a circumstance where the contract,
> the control actually says, "commercial producer"?
>
> J. Breglio: You can't do it.
>
> D. Dower: You can't do it. Thank you.
>
> J. Breglio: If you're using your own money.

IN THE INTERSECTION

> S. Frost: The [nonprofit] theater issues the contract.
>
> J. Breglio: Well, but also, the contract can say anything. But as long as it's in the theater's home and the theater is using its money and it's responsible—forget what you'd like to do—as a not-for-profit ... the IRS and the codes and regulations require that you control the use of your money, singlehandedly. You cannot permit the use of your funds to be controlled by any third party. And that means "mutual."
>
> ...
>
> L. Plotkin: But, John, what does it mean if you say that the not-for-profit has control, but [the commercial producer and nonprofit] have "mutual" control over the creative team, and most of these contracts provide that the nonprofit can't fire any of the creative team without the approval of the commercial producer?
>
> J. Breglio: If the not-for-profit is using its money, and I was representing that not-for-profit, I would prohibit them from signing that contract. That is directly opposed to the IRS regulations for the last twenty-five years. If it's your money you cannot lose control of ultimate decision making of how the money is used.

Breglio then gave an example of a nonprofit and a commercial producer entering into an agreement without the commercial producer being aware that the nonprofit had already made commitments to hire three directors for its season, meaning that the commercial producer would be required to hire one of those three directors. Being boxed into this decision made the commercial producer "furious" according to Breglio; but he pointed out that, legally, the producer had no recourse, as legally the nonprofit "needed to be able to make that decision."

Breglio then raised another area about which nonprofits and commercial producers sometimes clash—when to close a show.

J. Breglio: Many commercial producers who have given not-for-profits money want the show closed, because their money is being used up ... and the not-for-profit says, "No! We have a ten-week subscription. We're going to lose money. That's our mission." ... What is technically a "loss" against the profit producer who gave the money—that's the price you have to pay.

...

L. Plotkin: It really depends on where the line is drawn. It's a continuum. So while, in most cases, I don't see any control in the hands of the commercial producer as to the duration of the run after the contract is signed, it may be in the contract how long that run is going to be. But if it is not, then the not-for-profit has the ability to control the duration of the run.

M. David: ... We have had, in many of [our contracts], a clause which says, "in the extension, not your regular run, the decision needs the approval of both parties."

J. Breglio: That's fine because ... that does not give the commercial producer control over the not-for-profit's funds on that decision.

L. Plotkin: It requires consent. How is it different if it requires consent than firing of the director?

J. Breglio: It's not about consent. It's about—does the consenter's approval relate to an issue where the not-for-profit's money is at risk? ...

L. Plotkin: I think you could argue that it's at risk if it is unable to extend the run of a show that's enormously popular at its theater.

D. Dower: This is why we invited the attorneys.

Breglio then capped this part of the discussion stating that such clauses were common and that if the decision to limit the run were made up front, and if the nonprofit made the decision without any outside force, then it would not be a problem because, while it may have lost the opportunity for additional revenue by not extending, it would not have put its own money at risk.

Kevin McCollum then stepped in and pleaded that communicating on every issue up front is both necessary and legal, urged the room not to make conversation itself the problem, and opined, "We're all afraid of legalities. And they get in the way of practical collaboration."

Breglio countered that his main concern was not those in the room who were well-schooled on the legalities surrounding commercial/nonprofit partnerships and had the means to hire attorneys to help them sort through such issues; rather, he was concerned that commercial enhancement was beginning to be adopted by smaller nonprofit companies outside of New York that do not have "sophisticated representation" or "sophisticated boards" and "do not know what they can and cannot do from a legal point of view." He suggested that it would be helpful if someone, the NEA perhaps, could fund a handbook of some sort for these smaller nonprofits.

Rocco Landesman interjected to clarify that the NEA would not produce such a handbook because it "would be a primer for, in a sense, a commercial production"—a comment that elicited a good bit of laughter.

Dower asked Michael David what else the group should be looking at in the chart and David mentioned *Limiting Exposure* and *Access to Exposure*. Michael David explained that *Limiting Exposure* refers to the desire by commercial producers (generally) to limit newspaper coverage of the work by national critics. *Access to Exposure*, he explained, refers to providing access to the work on stage to commercial producers and potential investors—that is, complimentary tickets to see the production once it opens. He noted that both of these points were significant ones.

Enhancement Income: So Why is it Creeping Upwards?

David Dower then moved the conversation to the *Enhancement* row of the grid. Michael David's first comment was, "Did you notice ... that the dollars go up?" Dower asked, "Is that the cost of doing business in the field in general? Or what's happening that the numbers are going up?"

Michael David suggested that "things cost more" but also that the price going up was "part of the dance, too." He explained that nonprofits sometimes included total costs for the entire run of the production (as opposed to limiting costs to those required to mount the production) and commercial producers such as Dodger Theatricals had agreed at times to cover such costs. He reasoned, this "could be evidence of bad deal making, or something we really wanted to do, or what they needed. Each one of these is different and unique to the piece."

Later in the conversation, however, the issue would be raised again with the suggestion made that something else was driving up enhancement: dependence by nonprofits on the income to cover their general operating costs. The conversation on this topic, led by commercial producer Sue Frost, revealed some of the potential tradeoffs that nonprofits may feel compelled to make in exchange for what amounts to general operating support from commercial producers:

> S. Frost: Well, and [enhancement] also morphed from "we could use a couple hundred thousand dollars to help us with orchestrations" to "this will cost $2 million because we need to balance our budget."
>
> *[There is a general consensus across the room with this comment.]*
>
> S. Frost: That has to be said.
>
> R. Landesman: That *has* evolved that way.
>
> D. Dower: And is that what we're looking at? When we see these numbers we're looking at the change from "pay the direct cost here" to "solve some problem in my operating budget"?
>
> S. Frost: And when the commercial producer is solving a problem in your operation, then the commercial producer says, "Well, I'd like more

of a say then." And if they don't have the well established relationship that makes these partnerships fruitful and good for everybody—

Frost didn't finish the thought but the implication seemed clear—this is perhaps what causes deals to break down.

The Big River Model: A Sea Change or the Next Small Step in a Long Evolution?

Commercial producer Sue Frost then suggested that time be taken to examine the evolution of commercial enhancement, starting with *Big River* (generally acknowledged to be one of the first examples of the practice as it was subsequently modeled by the field):

> I would like to take advantage of Michael [David's] long history doing this. We've spent a lot of time today talking about how we got here from a not-for-profit point of view; and I think it's very important to talk about how this whole idea of commercial enhancement or commercial producers and this intersection actually has come about because it's not like it's always been there. And when you talk about why the numbers change and why the costs change, I think the relationships have changed. And I think you're a great person to start this conversation, Michael, because you guys [*referring to Michael David and Rocco Landesman*] really started this with *Big River*. And why did you? Why did that happen?

Michael David then clarified that there had been a prior production that was enhanced, *Lady from Dubuque*, produced by the Studio Arena Theatre in Buffalo, and that the theater lost its grant from the New York State Council on the Arts the subsequent year as a result of having taken commercial money. As he described it, "[NYSCA] punished them for shaking hands with the wrong people." Loren Plotkin also knew of a piece produced by the Studio Arena Theatre in Buffalo, *Sunset* (later called *Platinum*), which came to Broadway in the mid-70s with enhancement.

IN THE INTERSECTION

The conversation was then redirected back to *Big River*:

S. Frost: [*To Michael David and Rocco Landesman*] Why didn't you take that to Boston? Instead of ART, why didn't you take that to the Colonial?

M. David: We knew him! [*pointing to Bob Brustein*] And, I mean, it wasn't ready for anything. And we weren't either. We were dumb disciples of Bob Brustein. We didn't know.

…

R. Landesman: We were so naïve. [*Looking at the chart*] This was the worst deal we ever did.

M. David: It's terrible.

…

B. Brustein: This is important. *I never knew it was a deal!* I didn't know they owned the show. I thought he was giving me a play. [A good deal of laughter from the room.]

M. David: I do think that there is … tit for tat in this thing. We didn't put any money up. I mean, Bob did the show and basically he took the quantifiable risk. And we were all totally new, so in the end I think you may find that ART got more money, a larger piece of the future, than anything else on this list. I don't know that for sure, but I think so, because basically he didn't get a check, too. And it was a bad deal anyway. We flipped a coin on that deal; that was how it was solved.

Frost then reiterated her point that *Big River* represented a sea change in the way that commercial producers brought shows along. She described this new model as "a commercial producer going to a not-for-profit and saying, "We can work together and produce this show." Landesman added to Frost's description, "And here's a check! At La Jolla we wrote a check to the theater."

Breglio interjected that before *Big River* many shows had been produced by not-for-profits solely with their own money and then, after they were successful, moved by commercial producers. He later commented, "The evolution is the important issue." Landesman then raised another shift in practice that emerged with *Big River*, using the nonprofit run to help capitalize the run in New York:

> One thing we're not mentioning is that we used the production in La Jolla essentially to raise money to capitalize the Broadway production. We had people come to see it in droves with the idea that they might write a check. So it was really part of the commercial process, that run (then) in the not-for-profit theater. It was part of the capitalization of the show.

David Dower picked up on this point and made the connection to the situation with *Funny Girl*.

> D. Dower: So the distance, then, to where we are—why there's an empty chair here for Michael [Ritchie]—is that now the capitalization is part of the process of the nonprofit run.
>
> R. Landesman: And the capitalization is not $65,000 or $200,000.
>
> D. Dower: It's $12 million.
>
> M. David: But it's not the *amount*. It's the *intent*. ... Their intent was to do the old New Haven tryout at the Ahmanson. That's the problem. They had a date. They were going to go someplace. They were going to go to Broadway.
>
> R. Landesman: It's essentially a Broadway tryout.
>
> M. David: It was a Broadway tryout.

NYTW's Jim Nicola then joined the conversation, picking up on Frost's point, to ask when it had changed from "David Merrick conceiving of a project and … mounting it himself and going to New Haven, so that it was all in the commercial realm?" The group began to home in on what had changed in the environment for commercial producers that led to the "sea change" as Frost had characterized it:

> S. Frost: This was a different model. And it was an exciting model because a commercial production out of town was no longer affordable. It was no longer practical. You couldn't go and make mistakes out of town. It was too expensive. The physical production was too expensive.
>
> M. David: And Broadway became extraordinarily expensive, dangerous, unsupportive, unwelcoming. Shows are children. It was child abuse to take your child and basically attempt to give it a fair shake on Broadway.
>
> S. Frost: When you look at Broadway and what it cost in the early 70s to produce and what it cost in the late 70s to produce a show on Broadway—that's when it all went to hell in a hand basket. And there was no other way to create new work from a commercial point of view.
>
> M. David: Well, there were workshops and readings, but this was a beauty. As Kevin [McCollum] said, there were people there.
>
> K. McCollum: You had a paying audience.
>
> M. David: That was it.
>
> S. Frost: You didn't have workshops with your friends telling you it was good.
>
> R. Landesman: I'm investing to see the show in front of a paying audience.

IN THE INTERSECTION

> K. McCollum: And paying is so important.

David Dower then asked John Breglio whether access to a paying audience puts the nonprofit's money at risk in any way. Breglio responded, "It's not a problem."

While Frost held firm to her point that Dodger Theatricals had "broken the model," Breglio held firm to the perspective that the evolution was incremental. He mentioned that there had been different models over time, precursors to the *Big River* deal, and that "slowly the need to use (if I can use the word 'use') the not-for-profit to cut down the risk became a very, very interesting thing for the commercial producers." He said, "If you move all along this continuum, you get the ultimate issue of enhancement, which didn't really start until—I don't know—ten, twelve years ago."

Commenting on this evolution over time, Breglio remarked at one point, "And some people look at it as being invidious. But it wasn't invidious. It was powered by necessity."

David Dower later picked up on Breglio's comment that "this practice was powered by necessity," asking "on whose part?" Breglio responded, "Both sides." He elaborated saying that while the word used at the conference, *intersection*, suggested a crossing of purposes, he perceived that there was "a sort of a merger, more than ever before, of not-for-profits and the commercial sector trying to do … really good work." Breglio then raised another issue that he thought needed to be addressed, looping back to Brustein's concerns expressed earlier in the day—the *frequency* of the practice.

Breglio warned the group that, under the charter of every not-for-profit, the predominant activity of the organization cannot be one that "inures to the benefit of private individuals." He explained what this phrase meant in the context of the current conversation by giving what he described as a worst case example: a theater that used to do eight shows per season, never taking money from anybody, that fifteen years later does eight musicals and takes enhancement from a commercial producer on every show. He cautioned that such a scenario—a nonprofit theater turning itself, in essence, into "nothing more than a laboratory for commercial producers"—could result in the loss of a theater's nonprofit status if the IRS audited it.

The group then asked for clarification on what would be considered "predominant activity"? Breglio explained that defining "predominant activity" was something that lawyers, the courts, and the IRS do and that it does not imply simply "a majority" or "fifty percent." He stressed, however, that his concern went beyond the legal prescription to a moral dilemma:

> I think you've lost your soul if you're a not-for-profit and ... all you've done is eight musicals ... and taken money from eight commercial producers. ... It's more than just a legal issue. It goes to the heart of what a not-for-profit organization is. ... All I'm saying is it needs to be examined by boards. It needs to be examined by the artistic director.

Oskar Eustis suggested, however, that Breglio was "setting up a straw man" saying, "Nobody that we know of does that." Breglio agreed but countered, "It's a slippery slope."

On Trust Created and On Trust Betrayed: *Passing Strange* and *Great White Hope*

Earlier, in response to John Breglio's use of the term "invidious," producer Sue Frost had commented:

> There were relationships that were mutually beneficial and there were relationships where people were taking advantage of each other. ... And I think this goes right back to your point [*gesturing to John Breglio*]. A lot of people didn't really know what they were doing and they said, "Oh well, it worked for *Big River*, it'll work for me" without having any sense of the structure of a not-for-profit. ... Without having the benefit of a relationship with the person who's the artistic director. And that's how it sort of grew into a place where it became perceived as a bad thing, right?

IN THE INTERSECTION

Breglio added, "Unfortunately, the fact of the matter is, there aren't a lot of good producers."

David Dower asked for response from some nonprofit theaters and Oskar Eustis picked up on Sue Frost's comment on the importance of the relationship and linked it back to Tony Taccone's points from the previous session about co-productions with nonprofits, saying with regard to his experiences at The Public Theater:

> It never saves me a dime to do a co-production with another nonprofit. … The only reason I do a co-production with a nonprofit is because it is to the artistic advantage of the project to develop. Therefore, I've never done a co-production with a nonprofit where I don't have a fairly intimate degree of comfort with the artistic director. And, to me, that's part of the … conundrum about commercial producers: I've actually never had such a relationship in any extended way with a commercial producer.

While Eustis continued to express reservations about taking a project from a commercial producer, Molly Smith would later offer that Arena Stage *had* partnered with commercial producers, probably four different ways, and that it was the *idea* of each of the projects that had driven the collaboration. Christopher Ashley of La Jolla Playhouse also commented on Eustis's reservations that, from an artistic control standpoint, he found it curious that nonprofits were comfortable with the presenting model (taking work that was independently produced and finished before coming to the theater), but anxious about commercial collaborations. His own viewpoint was that "every single commercial producer/nonprofit relationship [had] more control than the presenting model."

Ashley further argued that in even nonprofit co-productions you can "have as many conversations as you want, but the first theater that does it has 90 percent of the control." Eustis disagreed, referencing his experience co-producing *Passing Strange* with Tony Taccone:

> *Passing Strange* opened at Berkeley, but I promise you Berkeley did not have 90 percent of the control over that. We really worked

closely on that for years. And we were all over that show at Berkeley, just as [Berkeley] continued to be involved with it in New York.

Kevin McCollum then asked Eustis and Taccone to discuss how the transfer of *Passing Strange* to Broadway worked. Eustis described the partnership with commercial producers Liz McCann and Gerry Schoenfeld:

> O. Eustis: It's actually pretty simple because that model to a certain extent worked perfectly. Because, in essence, Liz and Gerry were, as far as I was concerned, willing to allow me to continue to do what I'd been doing on the show. So, the show just kept getting better all the way until it closed on Broadway. We were not [general partners]; we had no liability in the show and very limited upside, almost none. But as a producing unit, as an artistic unit, we just kept right on going until Spike [Lee] called cut on the last day of the filming of it. And that was fantastic. But it also was one that was done—that show was done before Liz and Gerry saw it.
>
> M. David: It was the old model.
>
> O. Eustis: They shopped it.
>
> M. David: Shopping.

As the session began to wind down, Molly Smith offered up for consideration the possibility that all of this activity (nonprofits transferring shows to Broadway) had started with Arena Stage and its 1967 production of *Great White Hope*, which was the first example of a show originating at a nonprofit and being picked up and transferred to Broadway. Smith further suggested that Zelda Fichandler's experience with *Great White Hope* was why Fichandler now says, "Broadway: no."

Oskar Eustis asked Smith to elaborate on the last point. Dower then explained that Zelda Fichandler lost her entire company when *Great White Hope* moved to Broadway and that Arena Stage didn't get any money out of the deal. Dower would later mention as well that the original artistic ambition and idea were not upheld in the transfer: the Arena cast had sixty-seven actors while the Broadway production used fewer actors and the theater configuration was changed from in-the-round to proscenium.

Smith explained that following the experience of *Great White Hope*, Tom Fichandler (business manager for Arena Stage) ensured that if something moved, Arena would get money for it, and wondered aloud whether the origins of enhancement may have gone back to this rift. Frost added that, conversely, the commercial world then began to realize that resident theaters could be "a great resource for wonderful shows."

Losing the acting company to Broadway was not a problem unique to Arena Stage. As Bob Brustein commented, the same thing happened at Long Wharf when its production of *Long Day's Journey into Night* transferred to Broadway. Dower characterized the loss of the Arena company as "heartbreaking" and a "psychic blow" to Zelda Fichandler because the nonprofit theater had been created to be the *alternative* to Broadway and at the first opportunity everyone had abandoned the cause.

Are Nonprofits Standing on a Weak Moral High Ground?

Christopher Ashley came in at this point to offer a counter perspective on the move to New York: that having a new play go to Broadway is just about the only way for it to enter the canon and have a continued life. He elaborated:

> You have to be really successful in a tour around the nonprofits, hitting an Off-Broadway theater, winning the Pulitzer prize, or whatever—you have to really hit the jackpot in other ways if you're going to avoid New York and really have that play land, like go on to be produced for years and years. So I think it's a conundrum in producing new work of how do you give that play an ongoing life in this country without going to New York?

Oskar Eustis added that the actors in Zelda Fichandler's company didn't just leave for the glory, they left to make a living:

> I don't know what Zelda was paying at that time, but I promise she wasn't paying a good upper middle-class living to James Earl Jones and Jane Alexander. And, you know, the thing I feel that we have to negotiate with, and it's one of, I think, the dirty secrets of our movement (it's not a secret to us), is that this fantastic flowering of nonprofit art theaters across the country has produced thousands of middle-class jobs for artistic directors, executive directors, managing directors, development directors. ... How many artists are making a middle-class living in the nonprofit resident theater movement? It's really horrible. And that's the Achilles' heel of our movement. ... We've got to figure out some way to help realize artists' economic dreams if we're going to stay vital in their lives.

Because Michael David would not be present for the second day of the meeting, David Dower offered him the last word. The man who throughout the day had used words like "cigar chewing" and "enemy" and "devil" and "unworthy packhorse" to characterize commercial producers (in the eyes of nonprofits) used his remaining moments to challenge the pervasive sentiment that commercial producers are primarily motivated by money:

> I don't want to begin a discussion with the people in this room about who loves theater more. But I must say the sense you always get is that the nonprofits love it more, really. We're sort of the crass guys. We don't love the good stuff, we just love whatever will make money, and so I go to Oskar [Eustis]'s point. Where we work, this dangerous place, the work is unsteady, the pay is unsteady, there's no health insurance, no one has a 401(k), almost no maternity leave. We work to make a living too. ... We are the Rodney Dangerfields of this thing. We get no respect. [But] I think what you'll find is we're very similar in what we do. The fact is

you have a [play] development office. We want to develop plays too. Our mantra is we want to produce shows we want to see in a manner that doesn't embarrass our children. There's nothing about money in there at all. Money comes later because we've got to pay ourselves and all the people who are going to do this.

So I would suggest, and I'm not here to do it, but I'd love a nomenclature change. I think there's a better word for us than *commercial producers*. I don't know what it is. It could be anything. ... The current moniker reeks of only one corner of what we do; but our role in it, which touches everything like yours touches us, that deserves a better adjective.

There was a brief silence and then Bob Brustein suggested, with a smile, "*Serious* Commercial Producers!" Once again, everyone laughed as they headed off to coffee.

REFLECTION, REFRACTION, RESPONSE: ARTISTS PANEL

Moderated by Molly Smith

I think we all understand that there are certain desires on the part of a regional theater or a nonprofit theater in terms of the palatability of the work for a wider mass. ...To me that's as much a question of art as it is of structure.—Amy Freed

I think there's no one in here who's a commercial producer who's had more successes than flops. I like the action, I like to win in the action; but the fact is you mostly lose. And you lose for everybody. You're taking that playwright and their dream into this snake pit. And it is a snake pit.—Michael David

There is no protection from the buzz saw of capitalism.—Oskar Eustis

The last panel of the day was a discussion with the three playwrights that had been given three-year residencies at Arena Stage as part of the American Voices New Play Institute: Charles Randolph-Wright, Amy Freed, and Karen Zacarías. Arena's artistic director, Molly Smith, moderated the panel and began by reflecting a bit on the discussion up to this point. Like earlier comments by others, her reflections suggested that, in order to survive, nonprofit theaters may have had no choice but to let go of some of the ideals that the resident theater movement was established to pursue.

It's amazing to look back on the not-for-profit movement and to hear the ideals—and to have lived the ideals both at a theater I started in

Alaska (Perseverance Theater) and now here. So I've gone from small to very large. And what's interesting to me about it is—hearing and living these ideals—how much some of the ideals are *ideals*. I mean, quite frankly, to be in the theater you have to be scrappy. Right? And to be in the theater, whether you're in a small place or a large organization, it's always about survival in one form or another. So it's not surprising to me that all of these relationships have formed.

The Incomparable Playwright Residency Program at Arena

Smith then went on to describe the Playwright Residency Program at Arena, a program that, by all accounts, is in a league of its own in terms of the level of support it provides:

> So we have three artists here. They're all here at Arena Stage. They're on salary. They're on staff. They each have three years to be here at Arena. They are able to write whatever they want during that time. We're commissioning them to produce at least one of their plays. Some of their plays they may be writing for Arena, some for other people that are in this very room. They also have a young producer attached to them. We have a playwrights' house here.

She then asked each of the writers to speak, prompting them to reflect on what they understand, what makes them nervous, and what scares them to death. While the writers raised diverse points for discussion, each seemed compelled, as part of their reflections, to express gratitude for the exceptional opportunity to be part of the residency program at Arena:

> C.R. Wright: What's amazing is to actually be able to write whatever I want. For three years we get health care, we get a salary—which is unbelievable. ... I've had commissions; but a commission is enough to, you know, [*chuckling*] get you dinner. ... I mean, I've worked in both forms (the commercial and the not-for-profit world) and being able to create when I want to, how I want to, is an astonishing gift.

A. Freed: Before I get rattled and forget to say, the residency program here at Arena is profound on a kind of molecular level for somebody like me, … an unwieldy kind of writer for, certainly for the commercial theater, and even the nonprofit world. So to have a three-year gesture of faith is … certainly much different than a commission because, as you say [*to Charles*], a commission is spent before you get it. Three years is enough time to take a breath and ask the question we usually can't ask which is, "OK, I have the means. What is it that I intentionally, purposefully, fruitfully, want to bring to bear to my work now that I've got a little room to try that."

K. Zacarías: Um, there's absolutely no reason why I should be a playwright. I think the odds were completely against it. I'm a Latina mother of three living in Washington, DC. … How do we all end up here? How I ended up in a residency that's vibrant and exciting is still a conundrum to me and something I'm really grateful about.

Reflections from the Playwrights— "Entertainers in a Goya Court Portrait"

Molly Smith picked up on Charles Randolph-Wright's reference to the commercial world and asked him whether there was a difference for him working with one versus the other

C.R. Wright: Money

M. Smith: Money. Okay.

C.R. Wright: *You know.*

M. Smith: Is that the biggest difference?

C.R. Wright: I think so. When people kept mentioning, which I appreciated, today, about being comfortable … having a comfortable life … having to sustain what you do. I mean, I work in television and film and I always say that pays for my theater career.

IN THE INTERSECTION

> M. Smith: Yeah [*chuckling*].

> C.R. Wright: You know, because it is money that sustains you. So you have to take certain jobs (as a writer, as a director, whatever)—you have to take jobs that you may, perhaps, sometimes, not want to do. But how do you survive? So I think the difference is obviously you'll make more commercially, but creatively you're typically more fed in the not-for-profit world. So, it's sort of … that's the conundrum, I think, for artists.

The issue of the failure of the resident theater movement to provide a living wage to artists—and the necessity, therefore, to pursue work in the commercial realm would be raised again later in this session.

Amy Freed opened by saying that being in the room the past three hours had been fairly terrifying and that she had "started to feel like one of the entertainers in a Goya court portrait," partly because "what we do lends itself so badly to justification, explanation, or eloquence when confronted with the realities of what the effort is."

Smith later asked her to expound on this and she said:

> The way one has to think as a producer or an artistic director is, in a certain way, diametrically opposed to the things you cannot allow yourself to think about if you're trying to work on a play. … Playwriting is more an act of listening than it is of constructing. … It's a very sensitive tuning of the ear. … As everybody knows, once you get into the process of production, from the artistic standpoint, you're in a constant negotiation and dialogue with the forces that are coming in on that sort of tuning fork in your brain—that's dictating the sound of the play, or the intent, or the meaning of the piece. And from the time it's on the boards or in rehearsal, everything that you do is about the defense of the intention of the work. And so the playwright's action is basically to build a big fort around any instinct you might have. Because the only thing you've got, if you're lucky, is an instinct.

Freed made two other points. She first spoke about the challenges of working in a business that is personal relationship oriented and, specifically, the fear of being thought "difficult," which is "especially fatal if you're a female." She described having to negotiate throughout the process as a politician and thinking, "I've never expressed myself, not once, for two weeks. Is it now possible?" She said she felt empathy and sadness at hearing the nonprofit and commercial producers speak about the "tremendous effort that goes into getting work up," but then rejected the sentiment and said optimistically, "But we can't be sad! We have to work through this."

Randolph-Wright picked up on the sense of solidarity in Freed's comments and circled back to comments made in an earlier session about theater as a "tribe," suggesting that while the idea is an appealing one, too often minorities are not included in such tribes when the lines are drawn. He elaborated:

> I loved when you guys were talking about *Big River* and the idea of what I consider to be "your tribe" ... how those relationships turned into something spectacular. ... I think we now need to look at how do you foster these relationships? How do you get more people relating to each other that are different from you? You know, that are not all in the same little club. How do you open that up and see more types of people ... from different backgrounds ... and still have that tribe and those relationships—because those relationships are ... what make us comfortable to create. ...
>
> And I loved, Michael [David], when you were saying, "We love the theater!" I mean, because we forget that. ... What we all have to sacrifice to make it happen.

Smith responded, "Well, there's very much a sense in this room of people going toward a common goal."

The conversation with Karen Zacarías was intriguing in large part because her opening statements largely centered on the impossibility of her career as a playwright and her surprise that any of her plays had been produced. Describing her play about a seventeenth-century nun in Mexico she remarked, "That should have never been produced."

Gregory Mosher followed up a bit later and asked Zacarías what she meant when she said that various events that had occurred for her professionally never should have happened. The conversation then took a rather humorous turn as Zacarías sought to clarify why she had been surprised by her success as a playwright and others responded in kind.

> K. Zacarías: Yeah. Well. OK. I mean. I mean. I'm a writer of … *color*. I have three *kids*. And I'm trying to survive in the *theater*. … And I wrote about something that I *wanted* to write about. I mean, I wrote [these plays] at graduate school. Who goes to graduate school in playwriting and thinks they're going to have a living afterwards? …
>
> G. Mosher: So you were surprised you got any money at all?
>
> K. Zacarías: Yes, I was surprised. … I love that I can actively be a playwright every day, even if it means that I have to teach; and I used to have to write grants. I've never written in any other medium.
>
> [*Turning to Molly Smith*] I don't understand. [*Looking back at Gregory Mosher*] So, I don't know. [*Turning back to Molly Smith*] I'm sorry. I was just kind of interested … and baffled … and also grateful to all these people in the room—
>
> M. Smith: —that are making it happen.
>
> K. Zacarías: Yeah.
>
> M. Smith: Absolutely.
>
> C.R. Wright: And you were surprised that it got *produced*, right?

K. Zacarías: Oh! I mean, I'm always surprised I get produced. There should be no ... it's not ... I don't know if it's commercial. Are nuns from the seventeenth century in Mexico *commercial*?

D. Binder: I'm *always* surprised when I go to the theater, when I'm going to see a show, and there are *people* there!

[Lots of laughter in the room]

K. McCollum: In the commercial world, anything with a *nun* it, we think is commercial.

[More laughter]

Zacarías then said that she was curious about something. She said she had written nine musicals for children (mentioning that two were produced at South Coast Rep and La Jolla Playhouse), and that she had always wanted to write a musical for adults but that it seemed "impossible to get there." She said that at no point in the conversation earlier had she heard the word "playwright" and that there was no sense of "one person in a room who was alone writing." She continued, "Maybe that's why I feel shut out from that big musical world. ... I actually think we might all have something artistic to contribute, but I have no idea how to get into that business conversation."

Rocco Landesman spoke up first and described the "difference in light years" between plays and musicals from a commercial producer's perspective:

> A play is, essentially, a playwright, an idea, a play. Maybe a director would work with that playwright and possibly develop it, or once the play is written have suggestions. It's a very intimate thing. A musical is exactly the opposite. It's a huge collaboration. There's a book writer, but it's not about an individual sitting in a room with a play. It's something completely different. ... They're both

called theater—or one's called musical theater—but they don't have that much in common, at least from a producer's perspective. ... I, as a producer, I only love doing musicals because that's where a producer really has an effect—has impact.

Michael David tagged on to Landesman's point, "George Wolfe has said more than once, at his most dour, that playwrights get no respect but at least playwrights of plays are in control of their work; librettists are in service of a bigger thing."

Smith then prompted Zacarías to share more of her reflections from the afternoon's discussion and the conversation took a provocative turn. Zacarías began by saying that she had run a not-for-profit arts organization for twelve years and then said:

What nonprofits traffic in is "worthiness," [while for-profits traffic in profit] ... Nonprofits don't pay their employees very well, but they're changing the world so that should feed them in many ways. And I think that can be a troubling and twisted and sometimes exploitative place to be. And what I found really interesting with the first session was that there was so much *shame* in this room [from both sides].

There was a good bit of chuckling and harrumphing in the room at the last comment, but Zacarías continued. She said she found herself more forgiving of people in the room than they seemed to be of themselves. She said she recognized the difficulty of trying to guess what the American public wants and then talked about having had a fantastic time at *Rock of Ages* on Broadway but also loving Dostoyevsky's *Notes from the Underground* at Yale. Her point: having the diversity of the commercial and nonprofit theater is a good thing. She said she "moved to this country to have a lot of options" and ended saying:

I mean, I don't like *Two and a Half Men*, I don't understand why 17 million people watch it, but I don't want to destroy it. I *do* want to create another show, or ten other shows that make people wander away from it. But I don't think we need to destroy what a lot of people are enjoying.

Commercial producer David Binder picked up on Zacarías's comment about trying to predict what people will want to see and disagreed rather passionately, saying:

> I don't think that's actually what I'm in the business of doing *at all*. ... When Kevin [McCollum] and I went to see *De La Guarda* we were in another country and were like, "We love this! We want to do this!" It wasn't like, "We're doing this because we're predicting that this number of people are going to come." I mean, and that's why I kind of joke (but I'm kind of serious) when I say I walk in and I'm thrilled that there are nine people or 900 people there. ... I'm not in the prediction business. ... I'm doing it because I love it. I want to tell that story. I want to do that thing.

Landesman seconded Binder's passions and, turning the conversation back to the playwrights, said:

> What leaps off each one of you is how much you love what you're doing. ... And I would say, in that way, all of us are just like you. ... This is one field where passion really counts, where it really matters. My entire career, whatever career I've had, is not because I was smarter or worked harder. I wasn't smarter. I didn't work harder. It all came down because I thought Roger Miller was the greatest genius of American songwriting and I believed that with a fierce passion. I had that one passionate idea. And everything else came from that. ... No one would choose the careers that we have all had because they make any sense—because it's the best way to make a living or have security or any of the things that people normally look for when they set out to form their lives. It's all because we have a passion for what we're doing. And there's no distance between us on that, I think, at all.

IN THE INTERSECTION

Has Artistic Freedom in the Regions Decreased?

John Breglio then steered the conversation to the findings from the 2009 Theatre Development Fund publication, *Outrageous Fortune*. Breglio recalled reading in the book that the average salary of a successful playwright is $23,000 per year and that thousands more don't make any money. He relayed the finding that many playwrights working in the nonprofit realm perceived they had less freedom and often faced constraints on their work—no more than a few characters, no more than one set, work that will appeal to a broad audience—because of economic pressures on nonprofit theaters—in particular, pressure to attract larger audiences and earn greater revenues at the box office. He asked the playwrights in the room if they, or any writers they knew, had encountered such constraints.

All three playwrights acknowledged facing some limitations. Zacarías mentioned that all of the musicals for children that she had written have eight characters. She went on to say that the Arena fellowship was allowing her to consider work on a much larger canvas:

> It's allowing me to suddenly think out of the box that I didn't even realize I was thinking in. ... Thinking of twenty people, thinking of fifteen. And still another part of you thinking, "OK, maybe I'll do it with twelve just because I want it to have a life." I mean, that's honest. We're not always running around thinking creatively all the time. We have to think creatively with a practical side to it.

Amy Freed said that working in the regional theater had caused her work to shift but that this was not "because of the theater structure but because of the responsibility of dealing with a bigger audience." She elaborated:

> For me, as a playwright, that was where I felt that I sort of took a real turn. I was finally in the gladiatorial relationship with a big house ... and my playwriting had to change. ... To me it was a playwright and audience shift, rather than playwright and institutional structure. Having said that I know—I think we all understand—

that there are certain desires on the part of a regional theater or a nonprofit theater in terms of the palatability of the work for a wider mass. ... To me that's as much a question of art as it is of structure.

Later in the conversation, Kevin Moore at Theatre Communications Group (TCG), the national service organization for theaters, observed that "anytime you start to mass market anything it changes the nature of what it is." Moore suggested that many theaters have felt increasing pressure to get more people through the doors and that this has had an inevitable impact on programming. Based on his experiences as a managing director, he expressed concerns that programming in regional theaters was becoming more homogenous, or commercial, and less relevant to the local communities or regions in which theaters are based. Moore linked the lack of community relevance to another issue, diversity, noting that at a meeting attended by managing directors and production managers of seventy of the largest theaters in the United States two weeks prior, almost every person was white and middle-aged. He commented on the situation, "It does not reflect the world that we're living in these days. It doesn't reflect what is coming up. And it's a problem."

Along these same lines, in response to John Breglio's question about the constraints imposed on playwrights in the regions, Charles Randolph-Wright spoke in terms of being an artist of color and inevitably getting the one slot in February. He also spoke of "always thinking about what category you are placed in" and the necessity of fitting into a certain category in order to get produced. He once again referenced the Arena opportunity, acknowledging "how great it is once in awhile, not to have to think about that."

Is the Continued Life of Plays Always the Goal and Always a Good Thing?

At this juncture I made a comment that I had recently read a biography on Margo Jones (widely considered to be the founder of the resident theater movement) and was struck by two things: the fact that she had produced a significant number of new plays in her first several seasons and that there did not seem to be an expectation that all of the plays would go on to be produced elsewhere. I asked the playwrights if it felt like failure to them if a work was produced once and never again.

Karen Zacarías replied, "We work in a profession, I think we're the only profession in the world, where we're actively competing with dead people for a small number of slots." (I interjected that I thought it might be worse for composers.) However, Zacarías believed the idea that one play, performed once, for a particular group of people could be fulfilling if the group of people experienced a "communion" with the work.

Amy Freed suggested that it depended on the work and said that the goal was for the work to be realized:

> There are things that are joyful sketches (coming forth in a year) that are meant to live and die, and there are things that are big parts of what you feel like you have to say as a person. ... And to work three or four years on something ... to have that live and die on a premiere is tough. Especially because I think most of us would agree that what we're really happiest with is if the work feels like it got realized. And it doesn't always happen on the first production. So if it's realized then that's all one can hope for, and that's a satisfaction. But sometimes it takes a couple of shots before that happens.

I then circled back to something Christopher Ashley had said in an earlier session about wanting work to move to New York because, without that step, the work would probably not make it into the canon. I endeavored to parse out the distinction between selecting a work one believed in and (after it was produced) making the determination to move it to Broadway versus selecting plays to produce *because* they seem to have the potential to move. I fed back to the group that what I was picking up from the discussion was that there was increasing pressure for new works to move on and asked whether my interpretation was accurate. Christopher Ashley responded:

C. Ashley: I feel the opposites absolutely. I feel that nothing is more important than that it happen fully and wonderfully in my theater for my audience and that it fulfills itself as a play—like that is its own absolute end in itself. I *also* feel like I owe the writer a shot at having their play launch into a life where different directors will do different interpretations of it and where different audiences will get a chance to see it.

Referencing a seminal talk given by playwright Richard Nelson at an A.R.T./New York event Bob Brustein then suggested that regional theaters were no longer producing new plays and Sundance Theatre Lab's Mame Hunt offered a possible explanation for this.[16]

B. Brustein: Isn't it true that most theaters are not doing new plays anymore? That's what Richard Nelson's speech was about. This is obviously not one of those theaters—and I think most of the theaters represented here are not one of those theaters—but most of the theaters in this country are doing workshops, they're doing readings, but they're not doing new plays. They're not *producing* them anymore.

M. Hunt: It's the smallest audience.

Running into the Buzz Saw of the Commercial Theater

At this point Polly Carl, dramaturg and director of the American Voices New Play Institute (AVNPI), joined the conversation to share her troubling experiences working over the past year on plays that had attracted commercial producers and the toll that this had taken on the playwrights of two of those plays. Without giving any specifics of the productions, she relayed that in one instance the commercial production kept getting postponed because the "star casting kept falling apart" and the writer had been asking Carl's advice on whether to hold

---

[16]Richard Nelson's talk was given April 9, 2007, upon receipt of the PEN/Laura Pels Award, given annually to two American playwrights and can be accessed at http://www.pdc1.org/viewthisarticle.php?article=22

out indefinitely for the commercial production or go ahead and allow it to be produced at several regional theaters that had been pursuing the work. Carl said that it was incredibly difficult to know how to advise the artist because the artist was basically saying to her, "You know if I make the wrong choice I'm not going to have a livelihood for the next year."

In the second instance Carl said that taking a play commercially seemed to be great for the writer's financial livelihood but seemed to jeopardize the writer's relationship with the nonprofit theater that originally produced the play. Carl then stepped back and reflected on these situations and the role of the nonprofit theater saying:

> We want to help the writer take it to the next level, but actually, the next level—what does that mean? You know? What does it mean for the writer? What does it mean for their livelihood? What's our responsibility? ... Look, I'm not pointing any fingers at the commercial [theater]—I love the commercial theater too. ... I'm deciding to work in a not-for-profit because it's a value proposition for me. It's me saying, actually, I'm not going to make the most money I can. I have a belief in a value proposition. And that's an ethical principle about how I think about art and art being made. And that can't be about, you know, just *ticket sales*. ... So I feel a huge responsibility to those artists.

Oskar Eustis responded wearily:

> Well, you know, I feel like, Polly, what you're talking about is these writers running into the buzz saw of the commercial theater. And there is no protection from the buzz saw of capitalism. ... All we can do is figure out, as best we can, how to support one another, how to support the people we believe in, how to experiment.

He remarked that this part of the discussion reminded him why he has fought to be a general partner on shows that The Public moves commercially: so that he could "protect the writer." A bit later Kevin McCollum would advise Carl: "I would say, as I would say to anybody in this industry, if you have a guaranteed production somewhere, take it—because if it's good, it'll get to Broadway anyway." Christopher Ashley would push back on this last comment, however, saying:

> I think there's a certain kind of theater that should end up on Broadway if it's really good because it's truly mass appeal, and there's a certain kind of theater that's really good that should only ever play to 100 people because they're going to love it more than anything.

McCollum said he agreed with Ashley but, in this instance, was picking up on Carl's point that there was already commercial interest in the piece.

Cigar Chewers and 401(k) Holders: Different Rhythms Stemming from Different Risks

After listening to Polly Carl's experiences working with playwrights in the commercial arena, Berkeley Rep's Tony Taccone said, "You know, one of the things this points out is the fundamental, rhythmic difference between how organizations work—the rhythm, how they make choices, the planning processes." He noted that whenever Berkeley Rep had moved a show to New York he had encountered a different rhythm working with commercial producers. He elaborated on this and an interesting discussion ensued with Michael David about what motivates this different rhythm.

> T. Taccone: It's just when these guys ... decide to go, they go! And you are expected, often, sometimes as an artist, to drop what you're doing and just go and be available. And it's hard. It's hard to know how to negotiate that. And as a playwright you're caught in the middle because you're often caught between this deal of we'll wait ... And then, it's *not* happening, it's *not* happening, it's *not* happening ... It's *happening*. ... It's certainly not how we work in the regionals.

S. Frost: You usually control your environment. You control your venue.

T. Taccone: That's right.

M. David: You're also paid. Commercial producers don't get paid.

T. Taccone: That was not a pejorative comment.

M. David: ... The other reason I guess I quantify my love for this thing we're talking about is we risk our savings, our children's educations, health, houses, on what we do. We don't get paid. ... We are the responsible parents for this group of thespians, avid thespians like all of you in here, who won't get any money unless we ... deliver. And there's no *grant*. We don't get grants. ... Our culture is clearly effected by, you know, the fact that we're not surrounded by an institution—even one that may not pay you enough, but it pays you something. And you have health insurance.

B. Brustein: Michael, you get royalties.

M. David: No one produces in our world for a royalty. Our business is totally schizophrenic. I think there's no one in here who's a commercial producer who's had more successes than flops. ... You're playing in the big game. Now I like the game, I like the action, I like to win in the action. But the fact is you mostly lose. And you lose for everybody. You are, you know, you're taking that playwright and their dream into this snake pit. And it is a snake pit.

R. Landesman: And the two years while you're developing it you don't get paid.

M. David: We wait all the time. Patience is much more valuable than money in our business.

Taking Care of Playwrights: Where the Movement Failed

At one point in the discussion Kevin McCollum suggested that playwrights need to take care of themselves in this process by looking out for their intellectual property. McCollum said, "In the theater, the wonderful thing is, the copyright stays with the author" but "with copyright comes responsibility for your decision." He then turned to Charles Randolph-Wright and asked, "How much copyright do you own in your film and television stuff, that pays every bill?" Randolph-Wright shook his head and McCollum continued:

> *None.* Because the studio is motivated to invest because they have intellectual property and they know what to do with it—even if it's a B minus they can get it into your home for free and you have to watch it because they can sell what was written to some Procter & Gamble product. So we're in a very adult business. And you have to take responsibility for the assets you have. And writers own their work. Michael and I try to develop it, create it, hopefully shepherd it by getting it to market (which is not a bad word, which means *research*). ... At the end *you* own it. And that's *exciting*. ... I invest in writers and take them to lunch and take risks before there's any production. ... I'm not going to own the copyright, but I'm going to get the best out of that author; and then we might actually create something that people want to see. And then if people want to see it, the money is there. The money is the *tool*. It is not the *destination*.

Oskar Eustis then sparked a small debate with Gregory Mosher by making the case that artists are going into these commercial deals at a disadvantage, in large part because nonprofit theaters are not paying them a living wage. Eustis argued (as he would many more times) that nonprofit theaters and funders must address this "structural problem." Mosher, however, questioned why nonprofits needed funders to, in essence, do the right thing.

O. Eustis: Almost every playwright I know that doesn't have some incredible facility with television or film, or a rich spouse, or something else, is desperately worried about money. So they're going into all of these transactions unbelievably one down. It's not like they're equals in the marketplace with their "asset." ... And I feel like it is a huge indictment of all of us who are making salaries. ... I would love it if we could get every funder together and just say with the moral suasion, "You don't get any funding as a nonprofit theater unless you have artists on salary."

R. Landesman: I agree.

O. Eustis: Well, you know, why don't you just do that? ...Why don't we have programs to support artists—that make them *not free agents* in those lunches with you? We should be doing on the nonprofit side "our share" of taking care of artists so that the commercial side isn't the only side where you can make a great living.

G. Mosher: Well what's stopping us? Why do we have to wait for Rocco to solve this? I was at a TCG conference twenty years ago. I said that I thought that every theater should have a playwright on salary and they said, "Well, how much should they make?" And I said, "Well, why don't you pay them the same as you pay your development officer? If it's $18,000 pay them that. If it's $150,000, great!" And, literally, everyone burst out laughing. And here we are. ... *Sixty years*. Sixty years we've been talking about this! I mean, what is it going to *take* for this *movement*—

O. Eustis: Money.

G. Mosher: No! Not money! There's plenty of money!

[Oskar shakes his head no.]

R. Landesman: Well, Arena's now done it; maybe there will be another theater

...

G. Mosher: Exactly.

O. Eustis: And The Public.

G. Mosher: Yes!

M. Smith: Seattle's doing it too.

Karen Zacarías then made the point that not only did Arena Stage pay her to redevelop *The Book Club Play*, it produced the third production of the play, and opted out of taking any of the royalties. The conversation continued:

G. Mosher: Alright, that's all great. Look, obviously this is a good thing that's happening with you guys. I'm just saying, as a *movement*, we just have to start with the fact that this aspect of our movement failed. It just did. And now what are we going to do to fix it?

...

O. Eustis: Greg, I'm sorry. I was making a very concrete proposal, which I feel like you're trying to—

G. Mosher: I'm just trying to get things warmed up at the end of the day!

O. Eustis: What I propose is that the funding agencies of the nonprofit theaters and institutions in this country, all of which have enough money to pay large staffs (including ours) should be told that they will receive no more money unless they have an artist on salary.

G. Mosher: I agree with you.

[Clapping in the room.]

> O. Eustis: That's something *we* should do. That's not something *commercial* folks should do.
>
> G. Mosher: You're absolutely right.
>
> O. Eustis: Nonprofits, we know how to pay for this.
>
> G. Mosher: You weren't asking Rocco to *pay* for it—just to put the *heat* on.
>
> *[Eustis nods.]*

In the midst of the conversation between Eustis and Mosher, Mame Hunt from Sundance Theatre Lab opened up a provocative line of inquiry asking the commercial producers in the room if they had ever been "patrons of playwrights." It was, at first, unclear what she meant by this. Michael David replied that five of his ten shows were commissions, to which Hunt quipped, "I'm not talking about commissions. I'm talking about a *salary*." By this it seemed Hunt meant, for instance, if it took a writer a year to write a play would a commercial producer pay that writer the equivalent of a year's salary. Michael David then responded that there was a presumption underpinning Hunt's question that was incorrect because "the only producers that could possibly put artists on salary would be the four that currently have hits." Hunt reiterated her question:

> M. Hunt: I wanted to know if there was a *model*. I wanted to know if there was a model … for commercial producers to support, directly, playwrights. I just wanted to know if there was a model.
>
> K. McCollum: The *model* is, "I love the idea, here's some money! I want a draft in eight months. Is that good for you? … Great! … Terrific! … Here's twenty grand!"

J. Breglio: The guy who did this better than anyone was David Merrick who formed his own foundation. He gave support to playwrights who would never have been produced on Broadway. ...

Once More unto the Breach: The Loss of a Vibrant Commercial Off-Broadway Scene

John Breglio then reflected a bit on Polly Carl's experiences with Broadway, and the "major, major effect on this entire industry" of the loss in the commercial theater of "a really vibrant Off-Broadway." He continued:

J. Breglio: When we had an Off-Broadway scene, twenty, thirty years ago, it was a place for plays that really belonged Off-Broadway and not on 45th Street.

G. Mosher: Samuel Beckett, Harold Pinter—

J. Breglio: And those plays ran sometimes for two, three years, four years Off-Broadway.

D. Binder: Even fifteen years ago we had that.

J. Breglio: But it's gone. It's basically gone now. So what you have are these wonderful plays beginning in the not-for-profit arena and then suddenly the alternative is Broadway, which is not where it belongs. ... I have seen agents who are so determined to get their playwright onto Broadway that they ignore the other possibilities before the play.

[Many people agree with this statement.]

J. Breglio: And so what I think the not-for-profit group has to do is, again, come into the breach because we have two things: a not-for-profit somewhere and then Broadway. That can't exist for many plays. So what developed about ten years ago and was done a bit,

> but hasn't really taken flight, really, are more cooperative things with not-for-profits. ... Like August Wilson, whose plays would go into six or seven places and then go to Broadway. None of them made money, by the way, except for *Fences*. But that's OK. He was sort of the marvel in the regionals in many different ways.
>
> R. Landesman: I know. We did many of them. Not *Fences*.
>
> *[Laughter.]*
>
> J. Breglio: But for me that is a critical commercial development that has created a huge gap. And the danger of putting a playwright on Broadway when he is not really ready for it is devastating. It can hurt your career for a long time.

Before ending the session Molly Smith called on Sue Frost who had wanted to join the conversation earlier but didn't have the opportunity to comment. Frost spoke eloquently about the "treacherous nature of trying to commercially transfer a show" from both sides, nonprofit and commercial.

> I mean, my whole world is musical theater, and always has been, and musical theater writers, you know, Broadway is Mecca for them. And it's very hard to tell them that ... you need more time out here, out here, out here, if there's a commercial producer dangling a commercial production. And having been in your position for twenty years, where I was trying to help writers get their shows produced, and then thinking that, OK this is the best step because that's where you want to be, and then seeing it crash and burn ... I finally decided I couldn't be on that side of it anymore—that I had to be in an arena where I felt like I had more control over what that pipeline was going to be. Because the pipeline was so screwed up! And then, I'm in this arena and I see, "Oh, I get a lot more about what can go wrong." Because it's gone wrong, you know, and I've experienced it.

And, and I think part of the issue is, part of what we're addressing here is, the ability for each of us to understand what goes wrong and how it goes wrong. And if we were better communicators about it, with our artists, and with our partners, then maybe not so many things would go wrong. Because, God forbid, we'd learn from it, even fix it, and do it better the next time.

Molly Smith responded, "Well, that's a perfect way to end this session." David Dower brought the first day to a close saying, "Tomorrow when we sit around these conversation circles let's look at how it goes wrong from each of our perspectives. And listen to each other talk about how it goes wrong. And see what we can learn from that. That will be a very useful way to begin tomorrow."

DAY 2
ROUNDTABLE DISCUSSION #1:
COMMERCIAL PRODUCERS

Moderated by David Dower

> There's something disquieting about something going on here. And the disquieting thing is what I'm trying to get us to find.—David Dower

On the second day of *In the Intersection*, the meeting structure shifted from a panel/discussion format to a "fish bowl" process, which had been successfully employed at previous AVNPI meetings. The process entails configuring the chairs in the room as two concentric circles. A small group of participants comes to the inner circle for a discussion, which is observed by the remaining participants who form an outer "listening circle." As the name suggests, those in the outer circle are asked not to comment upon what they are hearing discussed. Likewise, those sitting in the inner circle are asked not to directly address anyone in the listening circle. The second day began with primarily commercial producers in the inner circle and others observing from the outer circle.

Moderator: David Dower, nonprofit producer
Producers: David Binder, John Breglio, Sue Frost, Margo Lion, Kevin McCollum
Nonprofits: Edgar Dobie (formerly a commercial producer)
Other: Loren Plotkin, attorney and Kevin Moore, service organization representative

As David Dower had suggested at the end of the first day, the goal of these first three sessions was to examine when, how, and why things go wrong with commercial/nonprofit partnerships from the perspectives of commercial producers, nonprofit producers, and artists.

Dower opened by asking the group whether anyone had thoughts as to a place to begin the discussion on where the commercial producers (or those they represent) run into trouble working with the nonprofit sector. While not present for the first day, commercial producer Margo Lion proposed the first topic of discussion: "the creative relationship" between nonprofits and commercial producers.

Spirit of Partnership, Good—Legal Partnership, Tricky

Margo Lion opened the conversation saying:

> It's important for a commercial producer to select [a nonprofit to work with] not just according to who has an open *slot*, and who has an appropriate space, and who has money (which, of course, is always a concern); but rather, who is going to be your … *creative partner* in this?

Lion stressed that, having come from the nonprofit world, she understood that nonprofits don't simply want to be "presenting organizations." Rather, she said, "they want to be involved with the making of the show." David Binder picked up on the distinction being made by Lion and contrasted the "completely hands-off" approach of Dodger Theatricals described the day prior by Michael David—an approach that was "very interesting" to Binder—with commercial producers that "literally move in." Lion responded that the relationship that she was striving for was "partnership" rather than either "move in" or "stay completely out."

Lion suggested that there were both benefits and challenges with partnership. She pointed out that what the nonprofit theaters can bring to the table is a more "objective point of view" (because they are "not *invested* in the same way" as the commercial producer) and asserted that such a perspective could be "helpful" or in some circumstances "could result in conflict." Later in the conversation Lion remarked that all her projects done in partnership with nonprofits had gone very well.

Kevin McCollum joined the conversation, commenting that describing deals between nonprofit theaters and commercial partners in terms of "what somebody does for somebody else" is problematic. He then said he wanted to make sure that Lion understood what she was saying, which he characterized as, "You're going to them with something you already *have*." He continued:

> You have *developed* something. ... Commercial producers are developing, much more perhaps than the not-for-profits realize, and we are looking [out] for the whole life of that show, and for as long as possible. And actually, our primary relationship is with the *author*. ... We're looking at hopefully a decade relationship with this project. So there's a difference when it is developed at the not-for-profit and they call you and say, "Hey, we think we have something here, would you like to come and see it, do you want to come to a rehearsal, would you like to be sent the script, you should keep your eye on this." ... And we have to, I think, be aware that there are two ways in which these relationships get formed.

It would become increasingly clear as the discussion continued over the course of the day that the ways these partnerships get formed matter a great deal.

David Dower noted that there also seemed to be a difference between formal and informal ways of working. David contrasted the terms of agreement covered on Michael David's chart versus "the dance" and the idea of the two parties achieving "partnership, consulting, and shared engagement" around the art. He asked John Breglio whether, from a legal perspective, "formal partnership" was a slippery slope.

Breglio commented that Lion's characterization of the relationship—the "spirit of partnership" from a nonlegal point of view—was fine, but cautioned the group that, indeed, it needed to be careful about using the word partnership in a *legal* sense. He continued:

> Terminology can get you in big trouble when you do these things because people can get very worried about, "Am I giving up too much, or not?" ... A lot of not-for-profits get very worried, scared, you know, when they see the money come in. They want it and they don't. They've heard the horror stories, or whatever. ... What Margo talks about as partnership is, from a nonlegal point of view, really the key today. Because no longer should there be conflict. We've really merged our interests and we *need* to merge our interests.

Relationships Built on Trust + Unsigned Contracts = Risk

John Breglio then expanded on the topic of the *spirit of partnership*. Speaking from his role as commercial producer, he said he had been developing a project over the past couple of years with a couple of not-for-profits, one of which "had the project" first. He then shared with the group, "Believe it or not—I'm a lawyer—I don't have a contract yet." He explained why:

> I decided that I was going to take my chances and have just the relationship. And I said, "I trust it's going to work out. These are people I've known for many, many years." And I didn't know the author. So I created the relationship with the author first. And I wanted to create trust. If you create the trust that you really believe in the piece, and everybody feels that way, that really goes a long way.

Breglio argued that nonprofits and commercial producers now "need each other because money is coming [from] nowhere else" and that, as a result, the commercial producer "has to establish trust." He acknowledged that, of course, he would need to sign a contract eventually and (harkening back to his comments from the day prior) stressed that certain constraints would come with taking that action:

> And I understand when I sign that contract I have to agree that the not-for-profit is going to have full legal control over the ultimate decisions when [the show is] in their home. It has to be. And I respect that and I know that. But it's going to be irrelevant in most cases. The best contracts are always the contracts you never had to look at again. That's to protect. And I respect the integrity of the not-for-profit institution; they need that for their own protection, OK? But that doesn't mean that every step of the way I'm not going to have a conversation. … And I will defer because I should defer. … So when it comes to the legal issue of "hands off," which is what Michael [David] was talking about, from a legal point of view, you can't expect the not-for-profit to defer to you or to give you control or whatever.

Breglio's further explanation of the purpose and ramifications of a signed contract seemed to echo references made the day prior to it being preferable or important for commercial producers to come to agreement with their nonprofit partners regarding the creative team "in the beginning"—*before* contracts were signed.

Returning to the question at the top of the session, "What goes wrong?" Breglio said that at the end of the contracts session he had asked Michael David if any of his deals had been "horror stories" and that David had said, "You know, they all were pretty good. They worked out." Breglio commented, "And that's a testament to him and to the partners he was working with." However, David Dower pushed on this a bit, saying that the *Funny Girl* situation struck him as "a horror story" from the nonprofit side of things and he wondered how it had derailed.

Sue Frost remarked that she had been talking with Christopher Ashley the day prior about the fact that these kinds of projects fall off the map all the time because "they don't have the money or the creative team falls apart." Frost characterized the *Funny Girl* situation as "particularly painful because they were so close to production. It was so visible. It had been announced for Broadway. And then it just collapsed." Commenting on the impact on the commercial side she asked, "How do you get that project back up and running? How much has already been spent? And how do you make your investors whole?"

Likewise, she relayed that in her conversation with Ashley he had wondered aloud, "How do we as a not-for-profit theater protect ourselves from this kind of thing? How do we protect ourselves … because it's *our* audiences and *our* local press?"

Attorney Loren Plotkin, picking up on Ashley's questions responded:

> I think the answer is that you can't really protect yourself. I think you can have a contract, and the contract can spell out consequences, and the commercial producer can forfeit some sums of money, but you can't force the commercial producer to bring you that show. And if you've taken the position that you're relying on a commercial producer for a show the best contract in the world cannot save that situation. Now, you know, there are ways to make you *more* whole than you would otherwise be, but you can never be whole.

Kevin McCollum returned to a point he made the day prior—that, increasingly, in order to get commitments from stars and investors for the out-of-town production, the commercial producer must be able to secure a Broadway theater and get commitments for the capital needed to finance not just the regional production but the Broadway production. Unfortunately, McCollum further explained, investors "leave the party" but don't have to call you and say, "You know I really don't have the backing to finance your show." He summarized this situation saying, "Everyone loves it over *lunch* but they don't love it over their *checkbook*."

A bit later it would become clear why this happens. McCollum pointed out that as these deals develop—as producers seek to line up the investors, the nonprofit partner, the Broadway venue, the casting, etc.—everyone is "extending great goodwill" but avoiding the "elephant in the room, which is that *nothing is signed*. Everything is about *intent*."

Listening to McCollum, Plotkin made the observation that a nonprofit's risk "seems to rise exponentially with the amount of money that they're expecting the commercial producer to raise."

A Sidebar on the Press: No Place to Fail

The discussion of press *In the Intersection* was a minor topic of its own. Picking up on Sue Frost's comments about the visibility of the *Funny Girl* collapse, Kevin McCollum noted that a show opening at a theater such as the Ahmanson (the venue for *Funny Girl* at Center Theatre Group) was virtually guaranteed to be reviewed by the national press. He maintained that increased press attention (and the possibility of a less-than-stellar review on the regional premiere) was yet another factor compelling some commercial producers to raise the money up front to capitalize the Broadway production. McCollum, however, seemed to disagree with such a strategy. He shared his personal perspective that "anytime you get information from the world at a lower threshold of cost, it is an opportunity to make the right decision or the wrong decision." He then added, "And I want as many opportunities [as possible] to make that decision."

There was also a brief exchange about national critics buying tickets and reviewing shows in the regions even when they had not been invited, prompting one commercial producer to later implore, "Where do you go that's safe to work on something anymore? Where do you go?"

Recalling the area of press exposure (mentioned the day prior by Michael David as a point of negotiation in his chart), David Binder offered that there were often "competing and different points of view about whether the press" should be invited to the regional premieres: commercial producers often did not want the press to be there while nonprofits would sometimes court the national press in an effort to achieve increased visibility for their institutions. Loren Plotkin agreed saying that a nonprofit could have "a totally different agenda than a commercial producer." Binder wondered whether it would be productive to come up with some general rules or guidelines on this area.

The press would return as a topic of conversation later in the day.

Head-On Collisions:
Loyalty to Project vs. Loyalty to Community

About midway through the session, David Dower remarked that a number of people attending the meeting had said to him, "What's the problem we're trying solve? What's the need for the conversation?" He suggested in response, "There's something disquieting about something going on here. And the disquieting thing is what I'm trying to get us to find." After a brief silence Edgar Dobie, executive director at Arena Stage (and formerly a commercial producer) spoke up. "Well, David," he said matter-of-factly, "our experiences in this intersection have been head-on collisions."

Dobie proceeded to describe a particular production Arena Stage had done in partnership with a commercial producer and the problems it encountered when a key member of the creative team left the project quite late in the pre-production process. The first issue concerned whether or not to postpone the project given the loss of one of the lead artists. The commercial producer was in favor of postponing the project; however, Arena Stage felt strongly that the project should go forward because it had an "obligation" to its subscribers. Expounding on the loyalty of the institution to its patrons, Dobie said:

> We actually convince them to spend eight or ten ... or twelve
> evenings with us. And we take that responsibility very seriously.
> And so when we put something on the playbill, we're actually driven
> by an imperative, which commercial producers are not always driven
> by, which is, "The show will go on and we will deliver the show."

Once the decision was made to try to continue with the production, another problem arose as the commercial producer endeavored to take on singlehandedly the task of identifying a replacement for the creative team. As Dobie described it, "We had to force our way into that discussion and say, 'Actually, this is a partnership. We're doing this show together. Our asses are on the line too. We have to be part of that discussion.'" In the end, the two parties found a replacement on which they could both agree; however, the holding pattern that resulted from the time spent coming to agreement on various fronts created yet a third issue: the temporary loss of the writer to another project and a compressed period of time for script development. The uncertainties and delays (most notably in receiving the final script) then put a strain on the casting and rehearsal process and other areas of the organization, as well.

Though Dobie felt the finished product was strong, it seemed that the project had taken a toll on the organization that Dobie could not justify. After recounting this cautionary tale, Dobie paused for a few seconds. Turning to the commercial producers seated at the table with him he then asked in an exasperated tone:

> Do you know what that *does*? Do you know what that does to an *institution*? Do you know what that does to a *staff*? Do you know what it does to the respect that they have for the *leadership*? Do you know what that does to *us*? It's *appalling*.

John Breglio inquired of Dobie how things would have been different if a commercial producer had *not* been involved—if this had been a project that Arena Stage had produced on its own. Dobie suggested that, for one, Arena would have had more control over the artistic process—it would have been able to better manage the creative team and make decisions on a faster timeline. He circled back to the issue of trust, which earlier had been heralded by commercial producers, saying, "So what happens, if you're a trusting partner in those relationships? ... You get burned! You can get burned because you cede that kind of control."

Having been a commercial producer, Dobie said that he recognized that sometimes the best thing for a project was to postpone, but implored the commercial producers to understand that if they enter into a relationship with a resident company that there is a "much stronger imperative" for that resident company to "actually get the show done."

Kevin McCollum then asked Dobie why Arena Stage had decided to do the project. Dobie made the case that the idea for the show (which came to Arena from the commercial producer) was a good fit with the institution: the creative team was made up of artists that Arena "had on a list," and the content of the show itself was highly relevant to the Washington, DC, community.

After listening to Dobie talk passionately about the importance of the relationship with the community that the nonprofit must safeguard, Margo Lion remarked:

> You've brought up an important issue, which is, you need to do the show. You've scheduled it. You've got it out there [for your audience and for the press]. From our perspective, the [commercial] partners' perspective, we're looking beyond that production. That is where our interests [may] conflict.

Picking up on Lion's reference to conflicting interests, Dower reminded the group that the day prior it had been suggested by someone that the commercial/nonprofit relationship being discussed by the group was a "merger" and not an "intersection." Dower then offered that Dobie's story would suggest otherwise—that the goals of nonprofits and commercial producers are *not* aligned, are *not* merging. McCollum disagreed and asserted that while the goals might be *different* that they need not necessarily be *competing*. Using words and gestures, Dower and McCollum then proceeded to describe the "intersection" from each of their perspectives. While Dower saw it as a crossroads, McCollum saw it as two lanes merging on a highway.

> D. Dower: I think that this is how we see that it is an intersection. ... [*To Kevin McCollum*] You're coming into the intersection trying to get information ... at a *lower cost*. ... And we have the nonprofit driving into the intersection, from its purpose and mission, and not talking about the long-term necessarily, but talking about the community, subscriptions. It's the long haul and information at a lower cost versus producing for your community.
>
> K. McCollum: They're not mutually exclusive. They're not mutually exclusive.
>
> D. Dower: I'm not saying they're mutually exclusive. I'm saying we're trying to get through the same intersection with different goals [*Using his hands makes a crossing gesture in the shape of an X*].

> K. McCollum: No, I think actually it's an on ramp, you're on the road for a bit, and then together for awhile ... I don't think it's this [*copying David's crossing gesture*]. I think it's—[*McCollum gestures as though showing two cars driving alongside each other on a highway and then one crossing in front and the other behind, and both continuing forward*].
>
> David Dower: So we're trying to get in the left lane and you're trying to get in the right lane [*David copies Kevin's gesture*].
>
> [*Laughter from the room.*]

Later in the session, however, one participant commented that what he found most disquieting was that audiences in many cases can no longer tell the difference between touring Broadway productions and those produced at regional theaters and suggested that the problem may be goals that are too *similar* rather than too *divergent*.

The Other Point of Impact and Pain: The Creative Team Serving Two Masters

Leaving the issue of commitment to community, Loren Plotkin returned to the other impact point mentioned by Edgar Dobie: artistic control. Referencing the hands-off process described by Michael David the day prior, Plotkin said:

> There's no way that a commercial producer can be completely hands off. ... I think that in most of the contracts that I've seen it is not up to the nonprofit theater to hire and fire creative personnel without the consent of the commercial producer. So, if you are in the midst of rehearsals, and the nonprofit says, "Well, we don't think this director is working out, we want to fire him," their hands are tied.

Plotkin called this "a great potential area of concern." John Breglio, picking up on Plotkin's concerns, said, "At the heart of it I think this is why these 'partnerships' can't work" and suggested that in exchange for taking advantage of the opportunity to work with a regional theater and produce a show for $300,000 rather than $3 million on Broadway, that the commercial producer had to give up certain things, such as control over casting. He cautioned:

> That first step has to be respected—in terms of the local community and the local production—or else you have 100 people telling every creative person their notes and how they should change the show and everything; and then you have chaos.

Likewise, Sue Frost characterized the issue of control over the creative team in the scenario described by Dobie as "really important" and cautioned that nonprofits and commercial producers can enter into a partnership with "the best of good intentions," but in the end the creative team is "sort of serving two masters." Echoing Michael David's comment the day prior that having a "destination" was the "great adulterator," she suggested that if a project comes from a commercial producer to a nonprofit institution, and there is a promise to go to New York, that this "two masters" issue becomes an even "trickier path, in many ways, to walk."

However, David Dower pushed back a bit on Frost's "servant of two masters" analogy. He asserted the commercial producer has more power over the creative team if Broadway is seen to be a possibility and that the metaphor only works if the two masters are perceived to be *equal*:

> I'm concerned that we seem to have accepted a set of false equivalencies here. ... The artists in that circumstance are making sure that [the commercial producer is] happy, because they're here for the long-term, as well. They're making sure that they're going to be on the ride when it gets to Broadway. They're cruising right through the intersection with their eyes straight on where [the commercial producer is] going ... less about where [the nonprofit] is going. And the serving of two masters actually only works if the masters are, in some way, equivalent, in this equation.

Dower asked the commercial producers whether they felt there was "true equivalency." Kevin McCollum responded that while John Breglio had used the term "our advantage" ("our" meaning commercial producers), he saw the advantage as *mutual*. He remarked that if it weren't of mutual advantage for both the commercial producer and the nonprofit, then the deal "shouldn't happen." He also observed that some nonprofits seem to learn through their experiences working with commercial producers and then change the rules going forward for how they will be willing to work on these deals.

Trying to Get at the Connective Tissue, the Sinewy Material Underpinning the Successes

Coming almost full circle, the conversation then returned to the importance of how the relationship begins and the idea of partnership. Sue Frost shared her ideal relationship:

> What I really want to figure out is how I as a commercial producer can work together with partners to take a show from idea to Broadway, or beyond. Or, not everything should go to Broadway. I wish there were other alternatives. I wish I could talk to a musical writer and their agent and say, "Please, can we find an alternative to Broadway because that's not where this show belongs," but that's a separate conversation.
>
> But I think that if you're coming in at the last minute with $12 million and ... the commercial producer and the institution have had no history on the project or on anything, it's a very different situation than if you can find a way to say, "You know what, we're both in love with this material now, and let's go into this for the long haul. And let's look at how we can develop this together—as *partners*."

Margo Lion then said: "But don't we do that? I mean, you did that with *Rent*, Kevin." Kevin McCollum then talked about his experience (with business partner Jeffrey Seller) working with New York Theatre Workshop (NYTW) on *Rent* saying, "It came through friendships."

Echoing Frost's invocation of love of the project, it was also clear that a deep commitment to the material and the artists had brought everyone together:

> I want to go back to *Rent*, though, because, what you need to understand is, you know, Jim [Nicola] had the material, fell in love with the material, even in its rawest, most unorganized yet inspired way. [We] saw the workshop [and] said here's the money so you can schedule it. ... What was great is we talked to Michael Greif, we talked to Jim, we had many conversations, and we chose each other at that moment. And we fulfilled every obligation ... *Rent* wouldn't be what it is without Jim's guidance. Because Michael's a great director but Jim also had tremendous passion, and Jeffrey [Seller] and I saw that, and we were so grateful.
>
> And, you know, the only way things get complicated is ... you always have to be careful of the successes ... the successes really can test relationships.

Lion shared her experience working on *Jelly's Last Jam* saying that she and Gordon Davidson (at Center Theatre Group) worked together the entire way through—"as partners" at each step. She reiterated the point she made at the top of the session that the most important decision of the commercial producer is with which nonprofit theater to work. "Are you going just because they have a slot? Are you going because they don't cost as much? You know, *why* are you going?"

Recalling another example of success, John Breglio described *A Chorus Line* as a show that "was created by trust between Joe Papp and Michael Bennett—two visionaries who looked at each other and trusted each other with no contracts." He continued:

> Here's a living example of the trust that you have to start with. And if it's not that—I don't care what the contracts are, I don't care what happens later on—then when you go to that crunch, you're going

to have problems. You will. And then people look at contracts. But that's not going to resolve, ultimately, how art gets done.

While Frost had earlier suggested that where projects get into trouble is when they try to simply replicate successes, like *Rent*, she now came back to these success stories and said, "We talked about *Big River*, we talked about [others]. I think, honestly, our job is to look at the successes and figure out how to …"

As Frost searched for words David Dower asked, "Yeah, what's the connective tissue?" The group mulled on the successes for a moment and then the conversation continued.

> M. Lion: It's also the difference in the material. I mean both *Rent* and *Jelly* … were not big Broadway shows. They weren't shows with big sets and a lot of costumes.
>
> K. McCollum: No stars.
>
> M. Lion: And they were also *new* people and they were breaking *new* territory.
>
> S. Frost: Right! Right! It's a *different* animal. That's what I'm talking about!

The session wound down and David Dower brought it to a close saying, "So, lots of things stirred up!" The commercial producers rejoined the listening circle while a group of nonprofit producers moved to the inner circle.

ROUNDTABLE DISCUSSION #2: NONPROFIT PRODUCERS

Moderated by David Dower

Now, listen, we're here together because we were on two different ships, they both hit icebergs, and we both jumped into the same life raft. We find ourselves in the same life raft together.—Tony Taccone

I worry a little bit we're in a system where we're waiting for these incredibly bright and ambitious colleagues in the commercial theater to bring us good ideas and they're kind of surfing around looking for a place to land these good ideas. And I think that's insidious.—Gregory Mosher

The deepest concern I have, from what I'm hearing, is the impact on the imagination, and the creation of work by an artist, in the frame. What the initiating frame is really determines things.—Jim Nicola

Moderator:	David Dower, nonprofit producer
Nonprofits:	Bob Brustein, Oskar Eustis, Mara Isaacs, Jim Nicola, Tony Taccone
Other:	Gregory Mosher, producer and director (former nonprofit artistic director)

Dower opened the second session, for which the nonprofit producers were seated in the inner circle, by noting that several nonprofit producers wanted at different points to jump into the discussion with the commercial producers and that he would "leave it to the person who jumps most definitively to get us started at this table."

Different Models, Different Theaters

The session started with Oskar Eustis suggesting that the group take time to clarify "the distinction of the different kinds of enhancement deals we're talking about," noting with regard to the *Funny Girl* model that "it's very different" from the models used for *Rent*, *Hairspray*, or *Jelly's Last Jam*. Eustis made the point that it *matters* how the project originates. He said that he and a commercial producer had run into problems once because there was some question about who brought the project to whom, and that they had stopped working together over the confusion. He capped the story saying, "I think that's actually a really big deal."

Eustis also asserted that when a commercial producer is financing a *revival*, producing it, and booking the production into a venue at a regional theater before going on to Broadway, it is different from the collaborations that get formed around *new* projects, which require serious developmental work. It is in the latter case, Eustis suggested, that nonprofits and commercial producers have the greatest dependency on each other and, therefore, encounter "the greatest possibility for difficulty."

However, before the topic of different models could be fully opened for discussion, Bob Brustein took the floor. Prefacing his comments with, "I think it's time to throw some chairs," Brustein provided a salvo on the fact that nonprofits were formed to be a different kind of theater: *alternatives* (not adjuncts) to the commercial theater. His comments further revealed a belief that the growth of some nonprofit theaters had made it difficult for them to fulfill this role.

> I tried yesterday in my fumbling way to give a history to this resident theater movement or the nonprofit theater movement; and, in every case, you may notice, the theater was created as an alternative—not an extension but an alternative—to the existing system. The existing system being the commercial Broadway system, which was function-

ing very well, very prosperously but it was leaving out something that these theaters felt had to be supplied—whether it was decentralization, whether it was more advanced, more difficult kind of work, more dynamic, more political, more radical, what have you.

Also it's true of all these theaters that ultimately they got absorbed into the system. That's the natural development of American life and American artistry. The advanced artist, the Samuel Beckett of the time who can't draw flies when he first starts writing, starts selling out at the Belasco. [Chekhov] was never a very popular playwright, but now he is. Now people go to Chekhov's plays and they're done commercially and what not.

What I'm trying to say is that there are certain *ideals* that were *constructed* for the nonprofit theater, which I have not heard a word about in the last two days. We all deviate from the ideals—ideals are meant to deviate from. But you have to know what they are in order to deviate from them. And what I'm not hearing is the fact that there *was* a time when we were *different theaters*, we did *different* things. We didn't join together to do the same things to please the largest number, to bring in the greatest amount of money, and the greatest subscribers. We did, as a nonprofit theater, most of us did these things because nobody else would do them! We did Robert Wilson, we did Andrei Serban ... Because Broadway wasn't going to do them! And they needed a voice! They needed an outlet. They needed a stage.

And they're not going to get that stage if we are thinking about filling our large buildings—and that's one of the problems I have. They're beautiful buildings, I adore them. They are handsome, architectural contributions to our culture. At the same time they produce certain problems. ... You have to fill it. You have to pay for it. ... The smaller buildings, the little ones, you know, the fifty-seat, sixty-seat houses, were the things that we were leading. We were doing much more adventurous work. We weren't worrying about finding partners from the commercial theater. And certainly the commercial theater was not thinking about finding partners with us. It was only when these certain things began to succeed, that we were doing, that we got these *looks*, and we got these alliances.

> Uh, and I, personally—not to beat my own drum (but of course I'm doing that)—tried all my life, forty-six years of running these theaters, to not have these relationships with commercial theater. We spoke about one yesterday. I didn't know that was a relationship. I swear to God. It was my friend Rocco Landesman, a former student and former friend.

The room burst into laughter at the last sentence and Brustein immediately recognized the unintended jab and clarified Landesman was a "current friend." Brustein's thoughts would echo throughout the conversation.

Is Partnership the Right Word to Describe the Relationship?

The word partnership was used throughout the two days to describe the relationship between nonprofit theaters and commercial producers. While John Breglio would caution in the first session of the day against using the word in a legal sense, in this session Bob Brustein seemed to bristle at the use of the word because of its business connotations. He commented, "Partnership is a *corporate* word. It's not an *artistic* word. Artists don't form partnerships. I mean, they form communities, collectives."

A bit later in the discussion, Gregory Mosher would also question the use of the word partnership, for yet another reason. Being admittedly hyperbolic, Mosher said that describing the relationship between nonprofit theaters and commercial producers as a partnership was like describing Kruschev and Ceaușescu as partners. Addressing the commercial producers in the listening circle he said, "You believe it's a partnership; but from where these people sit it's not a partnership—because you got an army and they don't." He then illustrated his point with an example drawn from his experience as a commercial producer working with a nonprofit to produce a new play that then transferred to Broadway. He said, "We used [the theater] to produce the play. We used them honorably and they got something out of it. But any idea that [the artistic director] was my partner is insane. That was my show."

Shared Artistic Ambitions and Financial Struggles but Different Values and Processes

Returning to the topic of differences between nonprofits and commercial producers, Oskar Eustis made the point that (unlike Edgar Dobie) he did not see the conflict as one between loyalty to project versus loyalty to community. Rather, he saw the potential conflict in terms of values; and he stressed, as a result, the importance of forming collaborations with people you know and trust.

> I feel like my job *is* the long view. ... I'm doing the same thing in a noncommercial way that a potential commercial partner is doing in a commercial way. ... We're both trying to produce the project! And I think the fact that we're trying to produce it with different hats on and with perhaps different—some different values—makes it a very tricky road. ... Relationships are so key to this and the question of where a project starts is so key.

McCarter Theatre's Mara Isaacs agreed that the process of developing and producing new plays becomes complicated when (nonprofit or commercial) partners are added to the table. Like Eustis, she acknowledged that her goal was to look out for the long-term best interests of the "art," but suggested that often partnerships (along with other factors) made this difficult—not least because evaluations of art are subjective and different producers often have different tastes and opinions about what a project needs. She ended saying:

> It sometimes feels that the right choice for the art is not necessarily the right choice for the box office or the right choice for the partnership. ... And then, of course, who's to say what's the right decision for the art?

Along these same lines, Gregory Mosher while agreeing with Oskar Eustis that "it's not necessarily different aims, because we're all trying to create great work," suggested that problems do arise at times because commercial producers are obligated to the central *artists* on a project and nonprofits are obligated to their *audiences*:

> You're working on a show and the commercial producer and the not-for-profit are working together, and the actor, director, some key player in all of it, her schedule changes. Well, the commercial producer is *obligated* to then change the schedule to accommodate the central artist. Or even if Jerry Robbins were to rise from the grave and you had a chance to get Jerry—it's your problem, you get rid of the other person, you get Jerry on your show, and that's that. But the obligation to the not-for-profit *audience* is to continue with it. "So what? It's Jerry Robbins, so what? There are plenty of other good directors. You know, that's fine. We'll continue." Both of those are absolutely defendable positions. But they are in conflict. And they come up a lot.

A bit later Eustis would attribute the success of the partnership on *Passing Strange* and other co-productions with Berkeley Rep to the quality of his relationship with Tony Taccone. Taccone agreed saying that he and Eustis rely on each other because they share "endemically and inherently some of the same values systems." He elaborated on how values come into play in working with commercial producers.

> I've been spending the last twenty-four hours here kind of reflecting on where I started and where I am now. And in terms of this issue of *values*, trying to understand how different and similar it is. ... There's a systemic issue, I think, in terms of how groups of people come together and interact. And what are the values that actually drive those collaborations? Obviously there's a shared project, which everybody believes in. Now, one thing I want to say is that my experience of working with people from the other world, those people who are "listening," has been largely positive. I've been impressed with how smart they are, how committed they are. *But* the values that they are pursuing are

not entirely the same as the values that Berkeley Rep is pursuing as an institution and the way we organize people around it.

Edgar [Dobie] said this very eloquently, I thought, when he said "we have a different living situation." The way we are structured, the way we are investing in people, is fundamentally different in some way, from the way a commercial production is organized. And sometimes it's antithetical. Trust really helps get over that. And the belief in the project really helps get over that. But when it doesn't go well, those values flare up as hot points.

And so, it comes down to these issues of what are my values? How have my values changed? And am I, in some ways rigorous enough with myself and as an institution about what we're doing?

After reflecting on the differences in values and processes that he perceived between nonprofits and commercial producers, Taccone provided a possible explanation, and powerful metaphor, for why these partnerships began and why they persist.

T. Taccone: Now, listen, we're here together because we were on two different ships, they both hit icebergs, and we both jumped into the same life raft. We find ourselves in the same life raft together. ...

M. Isaacs: There's a metaphor.

O. Eustis: And there's no oar!

T. Taccone: Exactly!

[Laughter from the room.]

T. Taccone: And this idea of a model. It's not like it's *going* to happen. It's *happened*. And so we're trying to describe what happened to us. And trying to exercise a little bit of consciousness about where we want to go. Is there a creative progressive place we can go

> together as a community, as a culture? Because individualism, fame, money, materialism lead one to another iceberg. But we all kind of need and want those things too; so it's a really tricky road.

Picking up on the comments around values by Brustein and Taccone, Molly Smith would later reflect, "I don't think it's unusual that we're having this kind of conversation now because theater has always been a reflection of the world. And this is the world. This is the world we are operating in." She characterized herself and others as "children of the not-for-profit movement," carrying the same values that Bob Brustein and Zelda Fichandler brought forward, yet grappling with *how* to move forward.

The Thin Lines Between Trust, Reliance, and Handing Over Responsibility for One's Mission

A bit later, Oskar Eustis returned to the subject of partnership built on trust and the issue of never having taken a project that was brought to him by a commercial producer. He asked those at the table that had done so to talk about "how that worked, when it worked, or how it didn't." He ended saying, "It's a barrier in my head but maybe I need to get over it."

David Dower then asked Tony Taccone if he would discuss *American Idiot*. Taccone obliged and described having had a conversation with a commercial producer who called to discuss a few projects. Taccone relayed that as soon as the producer mentioned the *American Idiot* project he knew instantly that it was a good fit for Berkeley Rep. From his perspective the match was an obvious one because Green Day was from Berkeley, Taccone loved the album, and (rather serendipitously) when Taccone's son first heard the album he had suggested to Taccone that it would make a great musical—so the idea had already been in the back of his mind. Taccone said that the commercial producer brought the project to Berkeley with the director, Michael Mayer, already attached. Taccone described it as a "really healthy relationship" in all ways *except* for marketing. In the marketing realm he characterized the commercial producers as "obsessive" and "insane" and "exerting energy on things that would make no difference." However, he also acknowledged that his organization learned things in the process of coordinating marketing with the commercial producers.

Returning to the reason the collaboration worked—the quality of the relationship—Taccone summed up:

> I thought the experience of working on *American Idiot* was really, really good. So. But that's because we agreed artistically. And I would never, ever go into any relationship with anybody that I didn't have a really, really strong admiration for and respect for what they're trying to do.

With regard to *Rent*, Jim Nicola said his relationship with Kevin McCollum and Jeffrey Seller was also great and, moreover, that he was happy to hand the marketing over to the commercial producers when the show transferred because he had no idea how to fill a house with a thousand seats. He explained that NYTW was in charge when the show was in its house; and likewise, when NYTW handed it over to the commercial producers, they were in charge. "We respected their decision making there; they respected our decision making here." Eustis then probed whether that meant that Nicola produced and cast the show and Nicola responded, "Absolutely." Eustis asked Taccone if the same was true of *American Idiot*. Taccone responded that he was there the whole time and that he did the casting with the director. Nicola then clarified that the *Rent* model and the *American Idiot* model were not the same because *Rent* started at NYTW.

Following up on Brustein's earlier comment, "My friend brought me the play," Gregory Mosher offered a different perspective on whether it mattered where the project idea originated. He said, "Pretty much everything I've ever produced, commercially or as a not-for-profit producer, somebody brought it to me. That's a common experience." He surmised that there was nothing wrong with projects coming from others, per se, but said he did worry nonprofits were becoming dependent on commercial producers for projects. He noted that

Taccone had the idea for *American Idiot* the musical but didn't act on it and cautioned:

> I worry a little bit we're in a system where we're waiting for these incredibly bright and ambitious colleagues in the commercial theater to bring us good ideas and they're kind of surfing around looking for a place to land these good ideas and I think that's insidious.

Eustis picked up on Mosher's comments about nonprofits waiting for commercial producers to bring them ideas and projects and suggested that, to their own detriment, the nonprofit sector was also passing off to the commercial sector the responsibility for supporting its artists.

> We have to figure out if we're actually going to be grownups in this profession. ... We have to figure out how we're going to help make possible a life for the artists. And a life of dignity. ... Part of it is delegating the ideas to commercial producers, which is disastrous; but it's also the question of saying, basically, well you guys support all our artists, OK? And then they'll slum and come work with us occasionally as long as you make a living for them. And that's also disastrous.

How the Possibility of Broadway Changes the Process and the Work

Raising a somewhat different concern, Jim Nicola introduced for discussion the effect of having a commercial partner on "the people who are making the work." He suggested that when it is understood a work is going to Broadway it has an "irrevocable impact on what the shape of that work is going to be that is unconscious on everybody's part." Nicola returned to the subject of *Rent*:

> I didn't even know about Kevin [McCollum's] and Jeffrey [Seller]'s relationship with Jonathan [Larson] until after the workshop. ... If I was to define [Jonathan's] aspiration: the first stage direction in the first draft was, "On stage there's a rock band and in the pit is a

full Broadway orchestra." And I thought, "Here is someone who is trying to come to terms with a tradition that he's proud of and wants to be part of, but he wants to blow it up and reinvent it for his time and his generation. And how do we help that happen? And let's get everything out of the way that's going to distract or predetermine things unconsciously." … We got a real long way down that road. I don't think it would have been the same if it had been clear from the start that we had people who were going to enable this moving to Broadway. I think it would have been a very different outcome.

At one point, Nicola asked Oskar Eustis and Tony Taccone whether they had in mind the goal of moving *Passing Strange* to Broadway when they were working on it and they both answered, "No." Nicola then said that it was projects like *A Chorus Line* and *Rent*, for which the producers had no expectation of moving them forward, that were the ones to "transform the form."

Eustis commented wryly, "There's not a moment that I think Michael Bennett was sitting in a room not thinking about going to Broadway. He was *Michael Bennett*." However, from the listening circle John Breglio was shaking his head no, suggesting that Bennett and Papp did *not* have their sights set on Broadway at the start.

Eustis also relayed an experience working with a show that transferred, illustrating how a show can be "affected and formed by the environment—by the producing arrangement in which it [is] created." Summing up, he said:

> O. Eustis: That was not a show that was created in a nonprofit environment and then moved to a commercial environment. That *became* a commercial show. Which is—

> T. Taccone: A different way of organizing people and relationships!

> J. Nicola: My concern, really, the deepest concern I have (from what I'm hearing) is the impact on the imagination and the creation of work by an artist in the frame. What the initiating frame is really determines things.

O. Eustis: Right. That's true.

Molly Smith agreed with others that once a project was known to be headed to Broadway it changed the process, most notably, the investment of the creative team in the local production and community. She elaborated:

> [*To Jim Nicola*] ... I think what you're saying is absolutely right, Jim. What happens in that case, as soon as people who are within the cast, or within the creative team, feel this sense of "and now it may go on," it changes. It changes. And that's the hardest part of it, because it moves out of, "we're part of this community" and moves into "and we're going to New York." So we're already past the community. That's a really hard question for us to constantly answer and to be able to say, "No. We're doing the best production here, in Washington."

Smith also acknowledged that Arena Stage had engaged in partnerships with several commercial producers and shared her thoughts on why a number had not worked out as well as Arena had hoped:

> I actually think that a core for that has to do with decision making. ... Who has the decision here? How does the mutual decision work? When does it tip its hand because of what's happening financially? When does it happen because of a particular influence on the project? And that's where, for me, the rubber hits the road. Because the commercial producer and the not-for-profit producer, we're actually all excited about the same project together. It's not like one is looking at it from an entirely different point of view. We're invested in story. And we've gone into projects with commercial producers because they have the rights to particular projects that I'm interested in ... because they have the relationship with that particular writer. ...

Agreeing with Smith, Taccone would later remark, "I think where [the relationship can be] problematic is the issue about who makes the decision, when, and who has the power to do that—which is why the contracts are really important." David Dower asked Smith and others whether they perceived there was a "tipping point" in terms of making decisions. Smith answered, "Yes" and Jim Nicola responded, "When it fails it's because that process is not correct."

Who Betrayed Whom First? Relationships with Press and Audiences

Picking up on the discussion about the nonprofit versus the commercial environment, Mara Isaacs said, "I think we can't have this conversation without talking about how we create safe environments and we can't talk about safe environments without somehow getting into this press problem." She elaborated on her point and the conversation took an interesting turn—to the subject of out of town tryouts, which one participant noted have never had a safe harbor from the press, and to the possibility that nonprofits may be losing their "safe environment" position because work in the intersection sometimes resembles the old Broadway tryout model.

> M. Isaacs: I don't know what to do about it, because we clearly have no control. But I would like to dispel any assumption by those who aren't in the not-for-profit theater that there is this general feeling among the not-for-profits that we want *The New York Times* at all of our theaters because that's not true.
>
> ...
>
> D. Dower: You're a commute away from it.
>
> M. Isaacs: Well, even at La Jolla. I mean, wherever! The point is that there's no longer a safe place to do the work and figure it out. You're exposed no matter where you are.

IN THE INTERSECTION

...

G. Mosher: Practically, I would say that there was never a safe space.

M. Isaacs: It was safer.

G. Mosher: Sure.

M. Isaacs: When you asked *The New York Times* not to come and they used to honor that.

G. Mosher: But Boston, Philadelphia, New Haven—it was not a safe space. If you were an out-of-town tryout in 1938, it was not a safe space.

B. Brustein: Out-of-town tryouts. But it was safe for nonprofit theaters. Walter Kerr stayed away for us.

G. Mosher: Oh, I thought the context here was that commercial producers were looking for a "safer space."

M. Isaacs: I'm talking about regional theaters.

G. Mosher: I agree with you.

M. Isaacs: We had a show last year. There was no commercial producer attached and we couldn't keep *The New York Times* away.

D. Dower: But to your point [*pointing to Mosher*], where we are actually in this intersection, ... the press having a say at an out-of-town tryout is the same as the press having a say at an enhanced regional production.

Brustein picked up on the topic of critics and reminded the room that the nonprofit theater has long needed but never had "repertory critics"—critics that would understand that the resident theater is trying to make its point through a season, not simply a single play. He ended saying: "We never educated the critics properly."

Brustein also picked up on Molly Smith's discussion of community saying that one of the big differences between the nonprofit and for profit realms is audience—in the nonprofit theater people come because they know you and have a sense of your aesthetic, and in the commercial theater people go because of word of mouth and terrific reviews. He suggested that audience as "part of the company" cannot be achieved when there is "collaboration between the commercial theater and the noncommercial theater."

Mara Isaacs, however, challenged Brustein's notion of audience saying that she no longer had the sense that audiences today in the not-for-profit theater were subscribing to an institutional vision because the culture is more transactional and the relationship to the theater was shifting to a show-by-show relationship. Molly Smith, echoing Isaacs's suggestion that the audience has become more segmented, shared that Arena Stage now has four audiences: Classics, African American Works, Special Projects (generally musicals), and New Plays (the smallest audience).

Akin to Dower's suggestion about the changing relationship with the press, Brustein agreed that the relationship was now more transactional but asserted that this shift was a *consequence* of a lack of institutional vision—a point with which Isaacs disagreed.

Money in the Intersection: Starving the Artists while Feeding the Beast?

David Dower resurrected the topic of institutional survival and Tony Taccone's "perfect metaphor of the life boat" and contrasted survival with the "fifty- or hundred-seat house model" that Brustein described and the current reality of what it takes to sustain an institution and, at one point, asked of the nonprofit producers, "How much is money what you're in the intersection for?"

While no one answered the question directly, the issue of money was discussed in a number of contexts. At one point Taccone reflected on the clarity and honesty around money in commercial partnerships and contrasted this relationship with philanthropy, which he said had fundamentally changed. "There is almost no philanthropy anymore in terms of just giving for the sense of well being. ... I mean, now people expect something." He made the point that it was actually a little more insidious to have a relationship with a donor who "doesn't want anything—except they call you and ask you for eight tickets to *Book of Mormon* next week!" The comment clearly hit home for the other nonprofit theaters.

Taccone also acknowledged that it was widely understood among nonprofit producers that it was cost effective for a commercial producer to come to a regional theater and try out the work with a nonprofit. Around this point the conversation turned to an enhancement deal that was understood to have happened at a theater not present at the meeting, whose name was not mentioned. The incident concerned a show that had a New York Off-Broadway tryout run that wasn't quite ready for Broadway. Evidently, a not-for-profit regional theater then courted the Broadway producer to do another pre-Broadway run at its theater out of town, making the case that actor contracts would be cheaper than in New York so the producer would save money. What made the scenario troubling was that the not-for-profit was understood to have replaced a show that was already planned for its season with this Broadway show.

Someone expressed that in all directions this scenario seemed to have been quite efficient for the producers—the Broadway producer saved money on actor contracts and the not-for-profit replaced a show it would have had to produce with a show coming from a Broadway producer— but that the artists in all directions seemed to have subsidized this effort. In particular the point was made that the actors in New York would have had no choice but to take the smaller weekly salaries in the regions or "get off the Broadway bus." A provocative conversation ensued:

> D. Dower: How does it relate to our nonprofit mission to be creating subsidy for the development of commercial work?

[Silence for four seconds]

B. Brustein: That's the corruption of the nonprofits. ...

[Silence for three seconds]

T. Taccone: Well, that story sounds loathsome to me.

M. Isaacs: Yeah.

...

G. Mosher: Well, that's why I called it a drug yesterday.

T. Taccone: Yeah. Absolutely.

D. Dower: Does it sound anomalous? Like, "Wow, that's the weirdest story. It never happened before and it will never happen again?" Does it sound like that?

M. Isaacs: It doesn't sound like that. But it's not—

T. Taccone: It sounds like it's bottom feeding on a new level. So it's not shocking but it's also horrific.

M. Isaacs: And counter to the success stories that I think we're trying to get out there, about where the collaboration comes together and makes sense.

Jim Nicola then offered another perspective, "We're all on lifeboats. We're doing what we need to, what we need to do to survive. And there could be the best of intentions. ... That theater made that choice in the pursuit of the longevity, of the longer view. ... The other thing I would say is boards are an issue in all of this because they *love* all of this."

Dower asked, "Why is the board even relevant to this?" To which one person rather wearily responded, "Oh my God!" Mara Isaacs stepped in to address the question. She prefaced her comments by saying that she didn't want to make vast generalizations because there were "good boards out there"—to which Jim Nicola added "and good board members." Isaacs then discussed the board's relevance to the intersection:

> M. Isaacs: What I have seen at more than one theater is this sort of growth, the definition of success, morphing. ... So many of the board members—who live in the world, who represent the world, which is growing to be more and more about profit and perceived success and numbers ... And this transactional culture that we're all moving toward, whether we like it or not, *that* is becoming the predominant lens through which the conversations about the vision of the organization [are] happening.

> T. Taccone: No question about it. Bob mentioned this use of the word partnership as an example of how the language of business and capital has completely moved into a position of supremacy, in terms of the conversations that are going on. And I think that this began with Ronald Reagan's election to the collapse of the Berlin wall and here we are. You know, there is no other currency of vocabulary than "business."

> O. Eustis: Absolutely.

> B. Brustein: The star moment of the nonprofit movement came, I think in the 80s or the 90s, when the board of Trinity Rep tried to fire Adrian Hall and he fired the board.

> Oskar Eustis: 80s.

> ...

> M. Isaacs: And nobody gives money anymore, as Tony [Taccone] said, without an expectation.

B. Brustein: So you have the John B. Smith production of *Medea*.

M. Isaacs: But John B. Smith doesn't want to support *Medea*. He wants to support the *Book of Mormon*.

O. Eustis: I can get him tickets.

[Laughter from the room.]

In the middle of this exchange, Gregory Mosher picked up on the reference to lifeboats and asked, "Are you suggesting that the ship went down?" The conversation continued:

J. Nicola: The ship is going down.

M. Isaacs: It's leaking.

K. Moore: I just heard it!

Everyone laughed as, indeed, at that very moment, a ship's foghorn could be heard in the distance.

Dower then raised another money issue for the group. He first recalled Michael David's observation from the day prior—that not-for-profit producers have salaries and, thus, are not in the same risk position as commercial producers and playwrights—which Eustis, Taccone, and Isaacs all acknowledged as "True." Dower then asked whether administrator salaries were in some way driving the need for the commercial co-productions. The group seemed confused by the question so Dower elaborated:

D. Dower: What we're hearing is, and correct me if I'm hearing it wrong, but what I'm hearing is that the model has gotten more expensive, where we're no longer able to do things like rely on John B. Smith to fund *Medea*, so we're no longer able to pay for the cost of our operation out of subscriptions. People aren't buying the whole thing. We're more dependent on single tickets. But that the business model has changed. The model's different. ... And in some ways it's about money. And in some ways the business model includes this kind of salary place. But, am I just forcing salaries?

B. Brustein: It's about politics too because what you're describing is also a different political system. You're describing a socialist collective system as opposed to a capitalist system. In other words, in the socialist collective system you have a certain safety net, which is your salary or your unemployment insurance or what have you; whereas, in a capitalist system it's, you know, you have to make your own way. And you can even make a killing. Or you can die, be killed. That's the difference. And it's a major difference when you put these two systems together.

O. Eustis: But, and this is what, for me, is the huge, *huge* weakness in the whole nonprofit ethos. Because the basic premise of this is we get *salaries*, we run *institutions*. I've never made a dime off of anything we've ever done commercially and I never will; but I'll also get a salary every week and I'll be fine. And that's worked out pretty well—but not for artists! And it's ... it's just ... it's wrong! I think it destabilizes everything. *It means that the people who we absolutely rely on to create the work that pays our salaries are not making a living from the nonprofit theater!* It's a huge problem.

And they're not making a living really in the commercial theater, for the most part, either. ... We're not supposed to be individual productions. We're not supposed to be entrepreneurial in the sense of "take your risk and maybe you make it, maybe you don't." We're supposed to be *institutions*. And yet when we're not supporting the *workers* [*bangs on table*] who are creating the work that makes those institutions—

G. Mosher: And "wrong" is the right word. It is wrong.

B. Brustein: Because there are no more resident companies! The resident companies supported the workers. And those have all collapsed and disintegrated.

O. Eustis: The playwrights never got that.

…

T. Taccone: I'd take a little bit of an exception to the resident company as being the answer because we're still paying actors. Resident company actors weren't paid that much and we're still paying actors the same qualitatively bad salary that we paid them all along. … It's just that the conjunction of pressures that are on these theaters' economics—some of it's the buildings, some of it's what it costs laborwise to just get shows up. I mean, I'm always *shocked* [*bangs on table*]—$300,000 to do a solo show and without a set! I mean, what are we doing? It always seems really difficult to actually make the numbers work and it gets harder every year, which is why we keep trying to find other pockets of money to sustain the so-called "product" that we have on stage. And we cut back and cut back and cut back until … what are you left with? So I think the feeding of the beast thing is a real thing.

One theater director then shared that at a long-range planning session the theater's managing director had asked rhetorically, "What if we created a plan that didn't depend on the continued existence of the institution?" and that just having the idea on the table for discussion was a liberating thing. Brustein responded to this saying, "I think you're absolutely right. I think the institution has to think about its … You know, it doesn't have to last forever." Another artistic director acknowledged feeling differently about this:

> My goal is both to try and make as excellent and clear as possible what that role is, but also to put it on an institutional footing so it can survive for a long time. Because I think it's important.

Participants were then given the opportunity to share reflections with each other in small breakout sessions for an hour, after which they returned for a full group discussion.

ROUNDTABLE DISCUSSION #3: ARTISTS AND OTHERS

Moderated by David Dower

> I'm so struck by the need for the not-for-profit to just get their house in order and decide what their value proposition is.—Polly Carl

> I mean, it's been the subject matter of our conversations: what is the role of the nonprofit?—Loren Plotkin

Moderator:	David Dower, nonprofit producer
Nonprofits:	Polly Carl and Mame Hunt
Producers:	David Binder
Artists:	Charles Randolph-Wright and Michael Friedman
Other:	Loren Plotkin, attorney and Rocco Landesman, chairman of the NEA

The third session on day two put primarily artists as well as those that might be considered artist representatives in the inner circle. David Dower began by noting some of the terms that he had heard in the previous sessions: values, idealism, partnership, and power. A bit later Landesman also reflected a bit on what he had heard in previous sessions. He said the analogy that Gregory Mosher had used (the commercial producer is Russia and the nonprofit is Romania) was an apt one: you "start down a slope where there's no longer even a balance

IN THE INTERSECTION

of power. There's no longer even a sense of a balanced venture." Landesman expressed concern about Loren Plotkin's observation that as "the numbers get big, as the potential payoff gets big, [the nonprofit] is in the increasingly compromised position."

Dower began the session by inviting Mame Hunt of Sundance Theatre Lab to talk about a topic the two had begun to discuss on a break: that several Sundance projects (including *Spring Awakening*, *Passing Strange*, and *Light in the Piazza*) had gone to Broadway, and the impact of this on her program.

Money or No Money, Broadway is a Goal because Broadway Equals Success

Mame Hunt began by making the point that despite the fact that Sundance had no *financial* relationship with the projects incubated in the Lab that eventually had Broadway runs, the projects had a profound impact on the Lab because they brought it "notoriety." Dower reflected back, "There's an imprimatur that has nothing to do with the money." Hunt agreed and further suggested that because there was not a financial return on the investments in Lab projects, this notoriety was particularly important in making a case for the program's ongoing existence. A bit later Loren Plotkin would pick up on Hunt's comments and tie them to a topic from his breakout session—the consequence of success for a nonprofit theater, saying:

> If the success is that the shows continue on, then what we're talking about, this partnership, becomes almost inevitable for some of the theaters, ... where success is characterized as "going on" after that theater.

Hunt suggested that the desire to move a show to New York was a very "West Coast phenomenon." She later shared that she had taken enhancement money twice when she was running the Magic Theatre, "a very small theater" located in the Bay Area of California, because she couldn't make payroll. Hunt drove home the point that commercial and nonprofit co-productions were not limited to the largest theaters saying, "It's happening at *all* levels. It's happening at all levels."

Rocco Landesman asked those at the table: "If you had more money to produce would you then not need the commercial sector? Is that problem [the need to form partnerships with commercial producers] immediately obviated?" Hunt and many voices responded, "No," and Plotkin began to explain to Landesman that the problem "doesn't go away because success is defined ..." and David Dower finished the sentence, "in other terms." Many people agreed. Landesman commented, "That's a scary thought."

Dower reflected back to the room that what he was hearing was that the relationship seemed to benefit both sides: commercial producers value the information that comes at a lower cost and nonprofits not only rely upon the income to fill the gap that is no longer filled by contributions, but are increasingly validated by success in the commercial realm.

Landesman pushed back, however, saying that he found it hard to believe that if the money problem were solved for nonprofits that they would continue to work with commercial producers. Loren Plotkin conceded that in the discussions in his breakout group "several of the artistic directors said that if the economics were not a problem that they would not be entering into these partnerships." He then added, "But the issue of how success is defined is also pervasive."

Playwright Charles Randolph-Wright shared his perception that some theaters seemed to have a mission to move shows and others did not. He suggested that nonprofit theaters perhaps need to be more transparent about which mission they have. Hunt responded that a theater is not allowed to say its mission is to move shows to New York; however, Plotkin made the point that regardless of whether it were expressed as such, if a theater's *implicit* mission were "to get shows moving on" it would affect the programming decisions.

Issues for Playwrights: Process, Power, Protection

Probing a bit on Plotkin's concerns about success being defined as moving shows to New York and the impact of this on nonprofits over time, Dower raised Christopher Ashley's acknowledgment from the day prior that he felt a responsibility to a long-term outcome for the artists he worked with. Dower asked, "Is this an appropriate thing for a not-for-profit?"

Polly Carl, echoing comments made in earlier sessions said, "Once you put the commercial specter in the room ... not only does that change the economic conversation, but it changes the conversation about the art." She elaborated, "If you do a show, on its own terms, and at the end of that show it feels like it has that potential that's a different proposition than 'Yeah! Let's take that baby to Broadway!'"

Carl gave an example of how commercial measures of success can alter the process and product. Without mentioning any names, she said that she had recently worked on a project that was going to transfer with the original cast from the regional production but an actor dropped out, which provided an opportunity to replace the role with a star. She elaborated:

> The minute one actor dropped out we started to look for a star. We weren't going to have a star. But we started looking for a star. But then we looked so long for a star that another actor dropped out. So now we had *two* opportunities for stars. [*Lots of laughter in the room.*] So you see what happens. And then we lost the show!

Shifting gears, Dower endeavored to get at the issue of balance of power and asked Michael Friedman, from the point of view of an artist that had worked on projects that had both commercial and nonprofit producers attached, what the reporting relationship had been. Friedman said it depended on the project, but noted that, generally speaking, someone (either the commercial producer or the nonprofit producer) was clearly "in the lead." He acknowledged, however, that the balance of power was "sometimes somewhere in between" the commercial producer and the nonprofit. He noted that this was something artists needed to figure out and negotiate up front. Charles Randolph-Wright also talked about negotiating relationships on projects with multiple producers, noting that the process sometimes took time away from working on the project itself.

Michael Friedman then contrasted the ambiguity and confusion he sometimes felt working with nonprofits with his experiences in the commercial sector and suggested that the relationship between an artist and a commercial producer was more straightforward and that a "bad relationship" generally came down to contracts—to something having been poorly negotiated. Charles Randolph-Wright agreed adding, "But you know what it is."

Friedman shared that one of the greatest frustrations for artists is "not understanding … and feeling like decisions get made that feel arbitrary—that might have been three years in the making, but you miss some of the linkages." He reiterated the need for more transparency from nonprofit theaters, in particular.

> Whenever somebody finally says, "We don't have the money to do that," it's an amazing thing to hear—because it's just a truth. Or, "That just doesn't work in the season because of *blank*." Or, "We were going to do it in the season but this happened." … The more you know the less weird you feel and vaguely put upon, or angry.

Friedman then raised another issue for playwrights, ownership of work, saying that while it may be less financially rewarding to a writer to maintain ownership of a project for as long as possible, it gives the writer more control and satisfaction. He reasoned, "Because I think that's what you have: that's your power. Your power is the show, right? That's really all you have."

And on the subject of relationships, Randolph-Wright returned to the topic of the "tribe." He said that he felt fortunate to have had friendships and relationships in the theater that led to work, but that his perception was that most artists of color did not have such relationships, in part because they were not graduating from Brown, Yale, or Juilliard.

Dower invited Rocco Landesman into the conversation and asked him to share some thoughts. Landesman went off on a small "rant" as he characterized it:

Whatever words are spoken to the contrary, as Zelda put it, the person paying the piper is calling the tune. And that has, I think, devastating consequences on the long-term for resident theaters. … So the more this wall is broken down, I think the greater the danger for the art and, you know, the poor playwright who's in the middle of this from the beginning. Everything is conspiring against the simple act of writing a play and putting it on in the most protected circumstance possible. You know, Richard Nelson gave that, I thought, very provocative and challenging talk about what happens to the playwright even when—forget the commercial producer!—even when he gets to the resident theater. With the dramaturgs, with the artistic directors, the presumption is for the playwright that the play is, of course, not complete or not ready, or not at the point it should be. So the playwright needs support and dramaturgical help and changes and mentoring. And then, of course, you get to the whole level of the potential commercial production, and the playwright is even further compromised. …

It's a highly fraught and dangerous terrain in which everyone, I think, in this room—and I'm complicit because *Big River* was the first, was the beginning of this whole thing—from the commercial producers to the resident theaters who cooperate with them, are complicit in what used to be a pretty straightforward thing, with a playwright writing a play and getting it done in a protective environment. It's a lot on me and I think everyone has got to look in the mirror and say what's my role in the corruption of what presumably would be a very straightforward artistic process by a playwright. End of rant.

Later in the conversation, David Binder picked up on the idea of how a work is changed or constrained not only when a commercial producer is attached, but also when it's in an institutional setting, and noted that some of the most distinctive theater work in the United States is happening neither on Broadway nor in resident theaters, but is being self-produced by artists in presenting houses, "where there's no major organizational hand on the work." He noted "how distinct and amazing, sometimes for worse and sometimes for much better" this work seems to be. Michael Friedman pointed out that the work Binder was referring to was "not in the intersection," and Binder rejoined:

> D. Binder: That's what I mean! ... *That's* interesting to me because that's often where some of the most interesting work is happening—*outside of all of our structures*!
>
> D. Dower: In another path.
>
> M. Friedman: It's just not a lucrative path. That's why I was saying it's not in the intersection. ... It's never going to make you a lot of money; but you can live.
>
> D. Binder: I'm not talking about money. I'm talking about distinct, unique work.

Along these same lines, Randolph-Wright later commented that the regional theater used to be a haven, a home where he had the freedom to do the work he wanted to do but that (the Arena residency aside) this was no longer the case. He lamented, "Theater used to be the place where we would tell stories that you [didn't] see anywhere else. ... I feel like we've lost that because all of us run somewhere else to get the money." In part because of the exodus of some of the most talented theater writers to Hollywood, Randolph-Wright asserted, stories on television are getting much better—the implication being that in addition to being financially more lucrative, Hollywood is becoming artistically more interesting for writers.

However, Michael Friedman responded differently to Landesman's reference to a protective environment. The idea of protecting the playwright worried him, he said, as it suggested that the ideal system is one that ends up infantilizing playwrights rather than *producing* them, which is what they really want:

> I get worried when we talk about protecting the playwright. ...
> I don't know what that means. If I'm being protected from Ben
> Brantley, that's one thing. If I'm being protected from dramaturgs,
> that scares me because my entire career is based on the love and care
> of good dramaturgs. And if I'm being protected from audiences,
> that's horrifying. ... What I want is to write a play and I want you
> guys to produce it. And actually I don't really care if you're mean,
> or even if you try to steal all my money (because I assume you
> should try to do that and I should fight back and we should argue).

Responding to Friedman's points, Dower characterized the playwright as an "unequal partner" and Friedman agreed saying, "*Not* an equal partner! Because the moment you have to talk about protecting the playwright you are talking about your invalid aunt, basically."

Mame Hunt then shared an anecdote about a leading play development organization, the O'Neill Center, whose founding director, according to Hunt, felt he had to run defense each summer in order to keep playwrights from being lured away from the Center (down to the beach) to have private conversations with the commercial producers who had come to see staged readings of their new works.

> Lloyd Richards had to start saying, "Don't walk to the beach with
> these writers. Do not walk down that hill." Because producers would
> come up from New York and say, "Can I talk to you?" and they would
> walk down that slope and by the time they came back they had a deal.
> And that changed the process! That radically changed the process.

Hunt admitted that at Sundance they also worry about producers joining in on the process—to the point that even when someone like Oskar Eustis (whom she characterized as a "dramaturg's dramaturg") comes to the Labs, it needs to be clarified up front that he is coming as a dramaturg and not as a producer.

A bit later, however, Polly Carl would reflect that what she was hearing from the artists was that they don't want this sort of protection from nonprofits—"If a playwright wants to go off with a commercial producer and they want to walk down the hill [at the O'Neill] they should go down the hill; that's their prerogative."

What Should Get Subsidized? What's the Right Economic Model?

Related to the topic of distinctive work, Rocco Landesman asked the group to reflect on whether, given limited resources and the original purpose and impulse of the resident theater movement, funders should stop supporting theaters that pursue partnerships with commercial producers. He asked whether funding should be restricted to theaters "that are doing their own work for their own audiences."

In response one person asked, "How will you know?" and suggested that nonprofits had "gotten very good at lying." The discussion then shifted to the production of *War Horse* at Lincoln Center Theater, the playbill for which lists the National Endowment for the Arts as a major supporter. While one participant noted that the production was also subsidized in England, another suggested that by the time Lincoln Center took the show it had been an established hit on the West End. As someone said, "You throw a rock in the theater district and you'd hit someone that would produce it." A question was asked but never answered: if there are plenty of commercial producers that could step in and produce that show, should it be receiving subsidies? However, someone else pointed out there was also a school of thought that said "the only measure for public funding should be artistic excellence—and *War Horse* is a great, wonderful, inventive play."

Dower then asked whether the research and development, pharmaceutical conversation had something to offer the sector in terms of an economic model? While Kevin McCollum, who first raised the analogy, was not at the table, Loren Plotkin did his best to explain it.

> L. Plotkin: I think what Kevin is saying is that like drug companies—although no one wants to be like a drug company, but the metaphor is strong—a commercial producer spends literally years, in the

musical realm, developing that musical. There's underlying rights that can take six months, a year and a half if you're dealing with a studio to get the right to do a musical based on a motion picture. And then you assemble the group. And no one else is choosing who the writer, composer, and lyricist are other than the producer. ... So, the producer, over the course of two or three or four years, is investing tens or hundreds of thousands of dollars in the creation of this group who will then go on to create the intellectual property, that hopefully will benefit everybody. And in the metaphor, the drug company gets a patent on that drug and benefits from that patent in the future, along with the scientists, perhaps, who …

D. Dower: The scientists who were the developers of the thing.

L. Plotkin: The scientists are the artists, and the drug company is the producer … And then perhaps the model that has existed is not the model that really should exist. There should be changes in that fundamental model in order to accommodate what the risks are with the investment of an enormous amount of time and money to create these properties.

M. Friedman: That's called television, right? …

L. Plotkin: No, no.

[Michael Friedman looks very surprised.]

It's not necessarily about control. It's not doing employments for hire. The artist can … have control of the work.

M. Friedman: But with drug companies, though, the scientist does not have control.

L. Plotkin: That's correct. If the drug company owns—

M. Freidman: So if we're talking about the drug company model—

L. Plotkin: But it's not. I don't think it's intended to be a television model.

Dower then made the analogy to Prilosec and suggested that most nonprofits think of themselves of being in the development end, but are not continuing the path and living in the market and reaping the benefits of the long-term financial success of the product. To which comment Michael Friedman said wryly, "I need a Prilosec now, I think."

Plotkin suggested that if a show originated with a nonprofit theater and had a long life, a nonprofit could have ongoing revenue streams (that is, *Rent*, *Chorus Line*, etc.). Dower then said that what he was hearing was that commercial producers also see "the development world as their place." Plotkin agreed saying, "Well, commercial producers are developing these properties." Dower wondered aloud whether the life raft that both the commercial and nonprofit theaters had jumped into was perhaps "development"—that both the nonprofit and commercial theaters were trying to occupy the same space around the development of new work.

Searching for the Nonprofit Theater's Value Proposition

About midway through the session, Polly Carl put a provocative idea on that table that was revisited by the group as the day continued. She said, "I'm so struck by the need for the not-for-profit to just get their house in order and decide what their value proposition is." She elaborated saying that what she was hearing was that commercial producers were equally passionate and well-intentioned and that what she felt coming from artists was confusion as to "where the not-for-profit stands." Carl referenced David's example of a nonprofit canceling a show in order to do a co-production with a commercial producer saying:

> Nobody understands how that fits into the not-for-profit. And I don't think the commercial sector can solve that. I think the commercial sector should do what it does—which is give money

> to artists and develop work and make really good work. ... We're taking a tax break and we should give that tax break back.

Rocco Landesman picked up on this last point (one that he has often made himself) and said, "If there's going to be any firewall or pushback or consciousness or awareness about this, it has to be on the other side. I agree: it has to be in the not-for-profit theater."

David Dower then asked about the potential impact of a firewall between the commercial and nonprofit theater. He asked whether there was work that would not happen if the intersection did not exist: whether something would be lost in the culture. Loren Plotkin pointed out that these were two different questions and then responded to them:

> L. Plotkin: Whether you lose something in the culture is your own value judgment.
>
> D. Dower: OK.
>
> L. Plotkin: I think that there is work where, if as a commercial producer you weren't confident enough to raise $10 to $15 million dollars to put on a musical, but you did have confidence to raise a half million or $750,000 to get a look at it at a regional theater, then that's something that might die if you didn't go to a regional theater to work on it.

Dower said he had been trying to figure out if there was a unique role for the nonprofit theater in this process and Plotkin replied in so many words that this seemed to be the topic of the day, "What is the role of the nonprofit?" Michael Friedman offered that producing plays that are only going to run for six weeks seemed to be a "truly unique and wonderful" role of the nonprofit theater. However, others at the table seemed to reject this as the primary role for nonprofit theaters.

Mame Hunt suggested that what makes nonprofits distinctive is that they have an ongoing relationship with artists over time, as opposed to commercial producers that are concerned with product. But Charles

Randolph-Wright noted that commercial producers also have long-term relationships with artists. Landesman mentioned that he had produced six or seven August Wilson plays (to which Mame Hunt replied that August Wilson was the exception to every rule). David Binder, however, agreed with Randolph-Wright and Landesman, noting that "every producer here has ongoing relationships with artists that they … go back to again and again." In response, Mame Hunt pressed her point:

M. Hunt: But is that your *primary* reason for being?

D. Binder: No, but I think it's part of …

M. Hunt: *That's* what I'm saying …

D. Binder: … what we do.

M. Hunt: Yeah, no, I'm not saying that you don't do it.

The conversation then took an interesting turn as Michael Friedman challenged Hunt's point by asking skeptically, "Is that the *Arena's* primary reason for being?" Thrown a bit by the question, Dower said:

D. Dower: Uh … I think … I mean organizations have different purposes. I'm not sure. That may be *Sundance*'s?

M. Hunt: Well, and it was the *Magic*'s.

Charles Randolph-Wright returned to the discussion around loyalty to audience and asserted that the relationship to community was unique to nonprofit regional theaters.

Dower then asked, "Is it just a legal difference? … Is everything really the same?" Polly Carl answered that she thought this was the real issue and that her breakout group observed that nonprofits and commercial producers were "not the same in mission, but perhaps more and more the same in practice." Along the same lines as Randolph-Wright, Carl said that the distinction she preferred to make was "that the not-for-profit is a value proposition to its *community*, which is more than selling tickets." She asserted that the value proposition of a commercial producer is to succeed and make money back for its investors; in contrast, nonprofits don't expect their investors to make their money back. "That's a different mission."

Echoing Carl's comments about similarities in practice, Landesman asserted that, in terms of result, "you can no longer tell the difference anymore." He raised as an example a particular season (when he was still a commercial producer) in which he produced the new Tony Kushner musical *Caroline, or Change* on Broadway, while a nonprofit theater in New York produced a Broadway revival of *The Pajama Game*.

From the listening circle Brustein called out to Landesman, "You should have been in the nonprofit theater!"

Brustein then returned to the subject of the pharmaceutical companies and said, "It struck me that there's almost an exact parallel that could be made, which I think points up some of the dangers that you're talking about: drug companies giving money not to scientists but to medical schools who then have their scientists produce the pharmaceutical, which then goes back to the drug companies, and they make their profit on it."

Dower said to Brustein, "You stay right there with that thought. It's time to go to the next session." Those in the inner circle were asked to join the outer circle for the last session of the day, which would be a full group discussion.

FULL GROUP DISCUSSION

Moderated by David Dower

We have to defend what we believe is right even if it's not the exact right historical moment.—Oskar Eustis

The idea of just making a value statement at all feels radical. One of the benefits of the movement is that there was an identity of every regional theater that was in concert or in sync or in dialogue with the geography and history of where we were. ... So the idea of reclaiming our identities as organizations is great.—Tony Taccone

The full group discussion picked up where the roundtable left off: with a discussion of relationships between pharmaceutical companies and research universities.

Searching for the Right Toolbox

David Dower opened the discussion by raising the example of Genentech, a highly profitable pharmaceutical company based in California, which was started by Herbert Boyer in 1976 while he was employed as a paid researcher and assistant professor at University of California San Francisco, a state-funded university where he continued to be on faculty until 1991. At first, many in the room vocalized expressions of skepticism about the comparison, including John Breglio, who cautioned that even using terminology such as "research and development" was dangerous and distorting.

However, Margo Lion seemed to find the analogy to be a fruitful one. She shared that a friend of hers had started a nonprofit organization, Stand Up to Cancer, where funding for scientists was dependent on collaboration among research laboratories, a practice that increased progress in fighting the disease. Given an aging population, she again suggested that the nonprofit and commercial theater might work together to find ways to engage younger and more diverse audiences.

Lion then questioned why the relationship needed to be adversarial. In a similar vein, Kevin McCollum later suggested to the group, "We all have to recognize why we do what we do … and try not to be offended by each other without investigating what our family of origin is."

Lion then questioned why there was an assumption that doing commercial deals compromised the missions of nonprofits. She made the point that doing a project with a commercial producer should not be interpreted to mean that a nonprofit's "whole mission" is to do commercial work; and, likewise, partnering with a nonprofit on a project doesn't mean that a commercial producer won't also produce shows for which there is no need for that nonprofit partner. She asserted that collaborations between commercial producers and nonprofit theaters are, at times, quite necessary and that they can be "wonderful, fertile, and productive"—if there is "transparency and respect" and if the material is appropriate for the artistic mission of the institution.

Likewise, Oskar Eustis would later reflect on the fact that collaborations such as the one at Genentech had arisen because the government recognized that they were necessary for scientific advances to be made:

> If you go back to Genentech—what capitalism has figured out is that medical advances, for example, cannot be simply left to the private sector. The national institute of health gives enormous amounts of money to nonprofit institutions (the universities) in order to fund the basic research. And they understand that those people will then own patents and will go on to make millions of dollars. That's OK. America needs the health advances. So we've got a system for doing that, through the NEH [National Endowment for the Humanities], through the universities.

A bit later in the conversation McCollum clarified his earlier analogy of theaters as creators and distributors of drugs saying, "I'm not trying to be a drug company. I'm trying to create the drug to effect change within communities, which is live storytelling." He explained that he had not used the pharmaceutical company comparison to elucidate issues of ownership; rather, he had used it to make two points: (1) Theater producers are selling a drug—"the ability to get the hair on the back of one's neck to stand up five times." Thus, to put shows together is a kind of "alchemy." (2) Because it is expensive and because the audience "is the catalyst to the alchemy," the process requires a beta test—for which "you need a community." However, McCollum's assessment was that theaters were not structured appropriately to pursue "that research and development model." He elaborated:

> The institutions themselves, and all the people who attach themselves to the show, are set up as a manufacturing agent. ... Tools a producer and a not-for-profit have are steeped in a manufacturing ethic, and yet the actual process we're in is research and development. And I think we get prickly with each other because I think we all want the same thing. We're here to effect thought and dialogue within communities of people. Call it Broadway, call it Off-Broadway, call it the Arena, call it your backyard and sandbox (which is how I first got into show business, in Hawaii—that's what I did, I put on plays in the sandbox).
> ... We just don't have the right toolbox though, most of the time, all of us. And we think it's each other that are providing it but we haven't developed the right toolbox. Because you try doing an original musical: APC. What does that mean, APC? Well, APC is the settlement of a lawsuit in 1980 as the tool to create commercial musicals. It makes no sense in today's world. But that's the only tool we're all willing to work with.[17]

---

[17] APC stands for Author Producer Contract. In 1985 the Dramatist Guild distributed new production contracts between authors and producers as negotiated by the League of American Theatres and Producers Inc. and The Dramatist Guild.

> ... Do we have the right toolbox to take the next step, whatever it is? Maybe it stays with the regionals, maybe it goes to Broadway, maybe it's thrown away, maybe you take it to television?

Gregory Mosher responded to McCollum's point about the field not having "quite the right tool," saying that he felt strongly that all the wisdom in the room would not be enough to solve the problem and that the group needed to be talking to younger theater makers—to people that are now the age that Zelda Fichandler and her peers were when they founded the resident theater movement. Mame Hunt agreed adding, "It's like the 60s. We have to build the tool."

Jim Nicola also responded to the toolbox idea asking whether there was some sort of relationship standard or understanding of expectations that could be evolved to deal with the work in the intersection. Dower picked up on the idea, noting the curiosity that everyone had shown the day prior when Michael David distributed his chart; however Nicola clarified that he wasn't referring to "contractual stuff"—rather, he was talking about "behavior."

Later McCollum responded to this point saying, "I don't think we can codify behavior." He mentioned that when he saw Michael David's chart the first thing he noticed was how little it had changed from the first deal to the last. Mosher, however, later speculated on what would occur if there *were* a Chinese wall between the nonprofit and commercial (disallowing, for instance, the taking of enhancement money):

> G. Mosher: What would happen? Well, the not-for-profits would have to say, "Do I really want to do this musical or did I just want to do it because—for the wrong reasons? And then what would happen to the commercial producers—because I hear Margo [Lion] when she says "Sometimes we would do things where we don't need you," which implies that sometimes you *do*—but we'd think of something new. It's America. The one thing we're good at is thinking of something new.

M. Hunt: Reinventing ourselves.

G. Mosher: And we would reinvent ourselves.

[Silence for several seconds.]

Going Back to Core Principles

After questioning the usefulness of the pharmaceutical analogy, John Breglio raised the suggestion made earlier in the day by Michael Friedman that a unique and wonderful role for nonprofit theaters is producing plays that have limited runs, saying:

> Producing plays that only run six weeks—there's a fabulous mission, because there's a mission that no commercial producer would ever do. And the whole point for not-for-profit organizations is to get tax-exempt status to do things that no commercial producer would ever do.

Rocco Landesman was quick to agree. Breglio then challenged the nonprofits in the room saying, "If you look at it in a pure sense, *that* way, you have to force yourself if you're a not-for-profit to go back to those core principles." Tony Taccone commented, "I think it's really interesting that only commercial people are saying that," and others agreed with him. Taccone continued:

> There is no theater in the country that does not interact with the marketplace. … And to make this distinction of saying it's on the nonprofits to clean up their act. I think there's been a confluence of opinions here that makes me feel like, wow, wait a minute, you're trying to remove us from our actual history, in terms of what we're supposed to respond to.

Breglio reiterated his point saying,

> I'm not talking at the practical level. … What I'm saying is, (if that's OK), is that in order to keep your mind straight, in order

> to be able to get up in the morning ... I think you have to keep coming down to some basic core principles, which have really nothing to do with acting as a commercial being. Because if you lose those basic underpinnings, it's over! It's over!

Without naming names Breglio then mentioned that he talked a few years back with a nonprofit theater director whose organization was in desperate shape financially and who was considering, as a solution, to program six shows with a view to their commercial potential and secure enhancement income on as many of them as possible. Breglio said that he thought to himself, "That organization probably has to end. It's no longer a not-for-profit organization. It shouldn't be around. Because that is not anything close to what its mission should be." While the example was an extreme one, Breglio seemed to be suggesting that there may be a tipping point at which the core values of a nonprofit organization are violated to the degree that closure is perhaps the ethical choice.

Jim Nicola then said that while he "would philosophically agree" with Breglio that "some not-for-profits drift away from the mission, or the mission becomes cloudy or corrupted in some way," he did not agree with the assessment that there should be changes in the tax law. He said he feared that such measures would suggest, "This mission is acceptable and this one is not. Or nothing that's popular can be done in a not-for-profit theater—it has to lose money to get a tax break." He ended saying, "I don't think that's the kind of theater I want to be part of. I want to talk to people. I want people to come to our theater. I want them to like walking in the door. Is that wrong?"

Molly Smith said she agreed with Jim but said that if you looked at the formation of nonprofit theaters that they "were created as educational organizations." She asserted that if there was no longer an educational through-line, ("education of not just young people but also of the audiences") then it might be reasonable to question whether a theater was still a nonprofit. She made the point that it was the educational mission that separated nonprofit from commercial theaters and that this mission was "different from the individual productions that were created."

Bob Brustein then piped up to challenge Taccone's notion that "the resident theater is primarily attached to the marketplace," saying, "If it is, it isn't the resident theater anymore." He suggested that there were two revenue options for theaters: finding public and private sources of support or "having enough faith in what you're doing that your audience will ultimately come *with* you and the box office will begin to help you in what *you* want to do not what *they want* you to do." He then shared a story from his time at Harvard saying that when he began in 1980 they had 13,000 subscribers, which grew to 14,000 in the second year. In the third year the theater produced a quite challenging season, which included (among other avant-garde works) Lee Breuer's *Lulu*, and lost half of the subscribers. He said the theater was never again able to build the subscriber base to more than 10,000 because they "never put on a play for the box office."

Brustein also identified another critical factor in the attrition of ART's subscribers. "They went to the Huntington. The Huntington was invented in that year to pick up the subscribers that we no longer had to please." Oskar Eustis chimed in, "Literally true."

Eustis then reflected at length on the role of the nonprofit theater vis-à-vis the marketplace and the challenges of upholding that role these days.

> The nonprofit theater is supposed to be a theater driven by values that are not determined by the marketplace. The commercial theater is supposed to be determined by the marketplace. That's the difference between the two. But it seems to me that we are operating within a cultural climate where the sources of support that are (again, throughout the culture) separate from the market, have been reduced dramatically. ...
>
> It's not just that the sources are gone. ... We are fighting against the current of history right now, to maintain, to establish and maintain alternative sets of value to the marketplace. We have to be smart about it. We have to be *Svejkian* about it (to quote my hero), which means that of course at times we need to collaborate with

> the marketplace because we need resources. ... But when we move so far that we are actually not using those resources to establish an alternate mode of value, but we're simply trying to be assimilated into the dominate mode of value, we've lost our legitimacy. And I agree, Jim, I don't think that there should be [changes to the] tax code ... because the federal government is too blunt an instrument at this point. There was a time when the agency that Dr. Landesman runs was actually a useful agency in terms of enforcing those things but it's too politicized at this point. Since the culture wars, it can't do it.

Eustis also talked passionately about wishing he could make all tickets at The Public Theater free (beyond those at Shakespeare in the Park), not only because of the benefit to the community but because he felt doing so made a very clear case for the need for funding. He acknowledged that free tickets would probably not be possible for all theaters.

David Dower then asked Eustis about whether he thought there was a set of values that could be built around the commercial/nonprofit intersection. Eustis replied:

> Well, the intersection is a little different. I guess what I'm saying is that most of what I'm thinking about is the nonprofit field. It's what we have to do to clean up our house—because good fences make good neighbors. I think if our house is clear, if our house is clean, it's going to be much easier for us to have a very productive relationship with our commercial friends, because it will be clear what we do and it will be clear what they do and we'll feel what our common ground is and we'll make appropriate contracts and we'll be rewarded for it.

A bit later Nicola revisited a subject he had raised the day prior—the decline in productions of plays of large size and ambition—saying, "There is a kind of *theater*, of a certain scale, that will make your hair stand up five or six times in an evening, that is *not* a musical, that is never going to be commercial, and that (to me) feels like the most threatened animal in our theatrical universe." A chorus of "Here, here!" and "Yes!" and "I agree!" followed.

Margo Lion then asked whether this wasn't one of the reasons that nonprofit theaters got involved with "these hybrid arrangements"—in order to have the funding to do more ambitious work. Eustis responded saying that Lee Breuer's *Lulu* would not have happened at American Repertory Theater if Joe Papp had not spent *Chorus Line* money supporting Mabou Mines for fifteen years. "That's one of the transactions that should work, when it works right," he added.

However, Mara Isaacs picked up on the example of *Chorus Line* royalties supporting Mabou Mines to point out that "the number of times that kind of money feeds back into the not-for-profit … is absolutely the exception and not the rule."

Sue Frost would later reflect on the different roles for the nonprofit and commercial theater sectors. On par with the analogies of the snake pit and buzz saw, Frost described taking young artists into the commercial arena as "throwing them to the wolves" and said that if an artist first had the opportunity to grow and see his work produced at a regional theater that he would be that much more equipped to face the wolves. She then turned to Kevin McCollum and said,

> You talked about R&D and you talked about manufacturing and we didn't talk about distribution. And I think that's the last step: the licensing, the money that comes back and then goes out to a much broader field. And I think that distribution becomes [the commercial theater's] responsibility. [The nonprofit and commercial theater] have to work together to keep all those different things happening. …

Reflecting back on Mame Hunt's question of whether there was a model for commercial producers to support artists, Frost then said:

> Because [the commercial theater is] really not in a position, Mame, to support an artist through their life. We're in a position to offer to take that artist and help them have a life.

IN THE INTERSECTION

A Call to Arms: Redrawing the Line

Amidst his salvo on the values distinct from the marketplace that were intended to underpin the nonprofit theater, Oskar Eustis suggested that what was needed was not punishment against those that do not uphold those values but rewards for those that do. He issued, in a sense, a call-to-arms, saying:

> What I feel like we are missing are strong, strident voices in the field, which I think could come from funders [or others …] to suggest *not* that there should be some legal punishment against nonprofit theaters that violate—but that we're going to attempt to steer as many rewards as possible to those theaters which are clearly manifesting in their work nonprofit values. …
>
> I mean, it's what Mac Lowry did! Mac Lowry got up on a soapbox and said there are certain things that should happen in this country and the Ford Foundation's going to put its money behind it. We need to find as many people who have some resources, who have some belief in something other than the marketplace, to band together and try to figure out how we're going to enforce that. …
>
> Of course, everybody will make their individual arrangements through the marketplace. We've got to get smarter about that. We're not opposed to each other, we share friendships and artists and tastes and all that. But it's the mission of the nonprofit that's the danger right now. That's the thing that's being eviscerated.

Mame Hunt then responded to Eustis's call-to-arms. She said her breakout group had talked about leadership and that she believed (particularly having run a small theater on the West Coast) that "if all of the LORT A theaters decided to lead the not-for-profit world in the [direction that Eustis was suggesting], everybody would go." She continued, saying that if especially those who started out in the trenches in small theaters that are now running major, successful theaters were to stand up and say, "We've got to clean up our houses" that leaders of smaller LORT theaters would do it. She then emphasized, "But they're not going to do it without somebody leading the charge."

Sighing and shaking his head, David Binder commented with wry certainty that the *commercial* theater was *never* going to have any leadership—a quip that drew significant affirming laughter from the room.

Gregory Mosher said that while he would like to think that what Mame Hunt suggested was true, his past experience was to the contrary. He shared that in 1987 Lincoln Center Theater (LCT) decided never to take artists royalties, even though it "seemed nuts" at the time, because it was their feeling that this was one of the things that should distinguish a nonprofit from a commercial theater. They assumed at the time that all the other nonprofit theaters would follow suit but it didn't work out that way. Oskar Eustis spoke up to suggest that others did follow, it simply took twenty years. He pointed out that LCT's "example was key to that."

However, a few participants expressed skepticism with regard to Mame Hunt's suggestion that LORT A theaters could or would lead the way, and Eustis asserted that the principled statement, if it were to be embraced, would have to come from some entity with credibility within the nonprofit field that controlled some funding.

Margo Lion then asked the nonprofits in the room if they had noticed a substantial decline in foundation and corporate support.

J. Nicola: Yes.

M. Lion: Like 30 percent?

K. Moore: At least.

M. Lion: At least 30 percent?

…

Well, I'm just wondering how practical, Oskar, the idea of looking for funding from other sources actually is. I mean, I agree with your model—I think it's a wonderful idea. But my question is: even with the appropriate and forceful leadership, a number of people in this room could provide, is it realistic to believe that you're going to be able to get that funding?

O. Eustis: Well, our funding hasn't really gone down. ... But for me it's not so much a question about adding funding. It's a question about setting up—(God, this sounds so pretentious)—setting up some kind of alternative pole to say, "This is the value system that deserves funding." ... That's what Mac Lowry did when he said, "This is what we're going to do at the Ford Foundation." The Ford Foundation gave an awful lot of money, but also what they did was Ford, along with the NEA, said, "You know what, America? This is something that deserves to happen." And funding flowed. Suddenly all these cities were competing for Tyrone Guthrie and Peter Zeisler to bring the Guthrie there.

M. Lion: It was a different moment.

O. Eustis: Of course it was a different moment. It was an easier moment. This is a harder moment. Just because it's a harder moment doesn't mean we're wrong. It means we have to fight. ... I mean, we have to defend what we believe is right even if it's not the exact right historical moment. ... We've been creative and entrepreneurial and we've been brilliant and flexible and theatrical in the last thirty years, but adjusting to the marketplace. I think we also need to put a big foot down and say, "No, we're not going to just adjust to the marketplace. We're going to insist there's something other than the marketplace." I don't know exactly how to do that.

Tony Taccone then responded, saying, "The idea of just making the value statement at all feels radical." He continued:

> One of the benefits of the regional theater movement, which I think has been maybe understated, is that there was an identity of every regional theater that was in concert or in sync or in dialogue with

> the geography and history of where we were. ... The increasing
> homogeneity of what the national season looks like—you know,
> it's become a national season! As opposed to a *regional* season.
> And I think that's a real loss. It's a real loss. And so the idea of
> reclaiming our identities as organizations is, I think, great.

Eustis returned to Mosher's idea about royalties and proposed that perhaps those that were currently not taking royalties should band together and challenge other theaters to do it as well, "because it's the right thing to do." He suggested that those unwilling to come on board could be asked to "write a mission statement as to why it's not the right thing to do" and that there could be a debate about the issue. He proposed artists on staff as another possible area to advance collectively. He ended by asking the group, "What if we try to take some principles and just challenge our field?"

Warning of a "real identity crisis," John Breglio responded to the conversation about reclaiming identity and endorsed the idea of, once again, clearly defining the distinction of what a not-for-profit theater is, particularly in the public's mind.

> So many people that I know in New York—do you really think
> they know the difference when they walk into American Airlines
> Theatre or the Colgate Theater on 45th Street? Not a second. Now,
> I'm not denigrating the Roundabout—it does wonderful work.
> But that's increasingly happening in a lot of other not-for-profit
> institutions or theaters. So, once you create that identity people sit
> back and say, "Oh, that *is* different from *Mama Mia*." And you do
> something different from *Spiderman*. And once that happens, you
> begin to identify philanthropic urges in people and then they really
> understand why they may have to give money to you as opposed to
> somebody who is doing what is clearly a more commercial prospect.

I spoke and questioned whether foundations should be given the charge of setting whatever line should clarify the values or purpose of the nonprofit resident theater movement. I returned to the biography of Margo Jones that I had mentioned earlier and said that I was intrigued by the fact that Margo Jones first wrote a manifesto that was then picked up and adapted by many other pioneers of the movement, whose activities eventually rose to the attention of Mac Lowry and garnered support from the Ford Foundation.

David Dower then asked whether it would be worthwhile for the commercial producers and nonprofit theaters in the room to create some sort of shared value statement "on behalf of art, or on behalf of the dignified life of artists?" The question was not immediately answered; however, a bit later Nicola wondered whether the relationship between the two sectors always had to be a "one-off" or whether arrangements could be made for parties to collaborate over a longer period of time over multiple projects, rather than "starting over again" every time there's a new project.

Towards the end of the session, Lion spoke up to say that she agreed with Nicola's idea of aiming for something longer term rather than "one-off" relationships. Lion added that she and the other commercial producers in the room had an aesthetic and a sort of audience that they were interested in and that the more nonprofits defined the kind of work they wanted to do the better such relationships would be.

Back to the Beast: The Things that Make it Hard to Go Back to First Principles

A bit later David Dower called on Edgar Dobie and asked if he wanted to share any thoughts. Dobie started by saying he grew up in Canada and that he didn't think there would be a commercial theater in Canada without the resident theater movement. Echoing the comments by Kevin Moore about the growth of the sector, Dobie pondered the enormous growth of both the institution where he now worked (which completed a massive building expansion in 2010) and in the number of theaters in Washington, DC, and wondered how all of this infrastructure could possibly be sustained.

I wake up every morning, come into work and think, "How are we going to keep the engine room going here?" We've probably bitten off more than we can chew. We've built a huge infrastructure. ... Washington alone went from—in sixty years—it went from the National Theater, which was shut down, to Zelda, to being now seventy-nine companies in this particular city. And I think there's probably not enough to support us all. And, I think we're all living in the same world and we're already seeing the unthinkable happen: we're seeing important resident theaters begin to disappear. And, you know what? [pause]. Maybe some of those institutions, their shadow shouldn't extend beyond the founders. ...

Our business model's broken. And, I guess, in the last decade we've tried to replace subsidy ... and I'm not sure that not-for-profit and for profit is the right way for us to be looking at ourselves. I think, actually, what the resident theater company needs, what the movement needs is subsidy. It actually doesn't need profit. I think if you use the word profit you should be defining it different ways, as Zelda said to us, a couple nights ago. ... Actually your purpose is—to pick up on your phrase, Kevin [McCollum]—is to tell important stories. It's actually one of the most generous things we do. We sit down and tell each other stories, whether it's around the fire or in a glorious arena stage like this, or in a Broadway house. ... And there are now nearly 2,000 theaters in this community spread across this country. ...

That's why we've got to really focus on what's of value to us. And if we do that, then I think we'll be in a much better position to have a healthy relationship with the commercial theater. ... All of us would love to have a *Chorus Line* in our life. All of us would love to have a *Rent* in our life. But those stories—we have to remember where they started from. They started from a very generous place. They started from a producer and an artist having an idea. I think we have to somehow get back to that. And Oskar, I think, you know that I agree with you on a lot of things, but I'm not sure that making

> all theater free is—that we're living in the right world and right environment to do that. ... I think free has no value.

Eustis responded, "Not to the people who line up for two days in the park to get their free tickets." Edgar acknowledged this but said that Arena's experience had been then when people "line up on the internet" for free tickets that they don't turn up to see the show.

Sue Frost was the first to respond to Dobie's challenges saying that if he was talking about seventy-nine theaters within a certain radius and a total audience of old white people (an audience that does not look like the world we're living in) that this *was* a problem.

> If we're not universally putting work out there that's broadening our audience and making theater more exciting for all people, then we can't survive. ... And I certainly think that theaters in their community, speaking to their community, trying to reach their community—and broadening that—only helps everybody. You know, it helps the work that we'd all like to do.

Kevin McCollum also asked, in light of the discussion on growth, whether the nonprofit theaters in the room were monitoring the gap between the highest and lowest paid person on their staffs to which everyone responded, "Yes."

Bob Brustein spoke up to share "a little more history," this time on the relatively short lives of many of the theaters that had the most impact on the American theater.

> The great theaters of the past, what we think of as the great American theaters, really lasted barely a second. The Federal Theatre was four years. The Group Theatre was nine years. The Provincetown Playhouse was eight years. I mean, this was no time at all; but they made their point in history. And that's the important thing.

I reflected upon the discussions about growth and buildings and wondered whether the group felt it was beneficial for organizations to own buildings or whether the sector would be better off with cities owning the buildings and leasing them to nonprofits for a dollar a year (The Public Theater model, as David Dower noted).

Eustis responded by contrasting the Eureka Theater, a theater where he and Tony Taccone "spent the formative years of their artistic lives" with The Public Theater. Eustis reminded the group that the Eureka Theater went out of existence and he suggested that this was right—that the theater had fulfilled its mission and promoted the artists and agenda that it had been created to promote. On the other hand, he suggested, institutions like Arena, The Public, and Lincoln Center need to be around permanently. He asserted that the building itself is not the problem; rather, to the degree that there is struggle, it should be over "what's *happening* in those buildings." He gave as an example the vibrant Berliner Ensemble saying, "For a century there's been fantastic theater in this building under every political regime imaginable—but the building stayed there. ... That's a resource that belongs to everybody. Molly doesn't own this building. I don't own The Public."

Bob Brustein joined in to say that as a founder he had it much easier than any of his successors.

> They labor under the initial vision of the theater. They labor
> under their own aesthetic and how they can correlate that with
> the initial vision. They labor under changing audiences and
> what have you. I think that makes major handicaps for people
> who are now leading theaters that were founded years go.

Gregory Mosher returned to the topic of survival and reminded his "commercial colleagues" that it is quite difficult "for a not-for-profit administration to reinvent itself." He elaborated:

> If, as a commercial producer you want to step back for two years
> and recharge, you can. But as you say [*motioning to* Edgar Dobie],
> six days a week, year in and year out, you get up and say, "How do
> I keep this thing afloat?" And Bernie and I fought over it—not

fought, but argued over it. He said, "Our job is to survive," and I would say, "Our job is to risk everything." And somehow or other in that dynamic we kept going in some way. But there's no shame in either walking away after seven years or having your board understand from the jump that every seven years we have to rethink why we're here and restate why we're here. And you can go back to first principles and adapt them. Or you can say, "New principles."

What Boards Have to Do with It: Embodying the Values of the World We Now Live In

Towards the end of the session, Kevin Moore returned to the subject of boards and suggested that they were an enormous, influential factor in everything that was being discussed. John Breglio picked up the ball and said:

> In our breakout we talked about it a bit. ... It's a real, major trend: a lot of board members, new board members, who have big check books, are completely uneducated about why they are there.

Someone mentioned that board members are often very encouraging of these commercial collaborations and raised the question of board members investing in shows and potentially receiving profits from them—a behavior that prompted John Breglio to quickly and strongly warn, "They can't do that." Rocco Landesman also spoke and mentioned that he had experienced in his current role as Chairman of the NEA how powerful it can be for someone from the outside to validate to a board what it should be doing.

David Binder then asked John Breglio to explain what factors had led boards to change. Breglio first reflected on the "slow evolution of successful musicals being the most prominent thing that's out there in the landscape of the theatrical universe." He commented that "creatures" like *Chorus Line* and *Rent* are incredibly "rare" but enormously successful, providing a flow of income that lessens the fundraising burden for board members.

Breglio then suggested that nonprofit theaters have ended up where they are now for several reasons. First, board members began to see more and more commercial activity taking place and, moreover, rewards coming to other organizations engaged in such behavior; then board members became confused as to the purpose of the nonprofit, and began to think that such behavior was acceptable or even preferred; and finally, board members began encouraging the behavior in the organizations on whose boards they served. Breglio offered sympathetically that it is difficult for nonprofit managers to say "no" to commercial activity when it is being encouraged by a board member that has just made a large donation.

Taccone disagreed with Breglio on two of his points. First, he suggested it's not hard to discourage a board member that is pushing you off-mission: "You just tell them, 'No!'" He then continued saying that it's the job of management to educate board members about the mission of the organizations *before* they get on board. He said that educating the board "requires a vigilance and kind of attention that many of us feel we don't want to give to it. ... It's constant." Jim Nicola chimed in agreeing with both Taccone and Landesman saying, "Three board members leave, three new ones come and it never stops. And it is very effective to have outside validation."

Taccone also asserted that the problem was perhaps bigger than Breglio described. Echoing comments by Mara Isaacs and others, he said: "It's cultural. These are people who live in this world. They have no idea about philanthropy."

Kevin McCollum agreed and commented on something else that had changed over time: there was a time when corporations would designate key employees to sit on the boards of local nonprofits, including theaters, because they were perceived to play a critical role in making a city vibrant—amenities that helped to attract employees to the city. He suggested that this was no longer happening—a point that was confirmed by others. But as Michael Friedman added, "I think it's important to remember it's not just a theater problem."

Around this point in the conversation there was a brief break, following which David Dower picked up on the recurring discussion around a values statement and suggested, as an alternative to a wrap-up session, that the group try to generate some thoughts on what might be included in some sort of statement to guide collaborations between commercial producers and nonprofits. An explanation of the exercise, the ideas subsequently proposed by participants, and brief comments made about those ideas, have been consolidated into a final section of this report. The following full group discussions occurred during and after that exercise.

Commercial Producers Seeking Out Nonprofits: Why Do They Do It? Is It a Problem?

Picking up on the recurring discussion around the lost value proposition of the nonprofit theater, commercial producer Sue Frost said she would hate to see the whole meeting boiled down to nonprofits needing to get their "shit together." She reiterated that there will have been no point to the meeting if nonprofits and commercial producers were not examining how they could work together to solve problems such as compensation for artists or building new audiences.

Margo Lion then revisited two points she had made earlier: (1) she doesn't bring to nonprofits projects that she can originate commercially and that she seeks out nonprofits when the piece is "more dangerous" or is trying to break new ground in one way or another…thematically or stylistically and (2) that in order to determine whether a nonprofit will be "the right fit" it's important to have a clear sense of that theater's identity.

David Dower asked Lion to expand a bit on the differences between projects that can originate commercially versus those that need to start with a nonprofit partner. Margo explained that she would probably go to a nonprofit if she were producing a musical with "unknown artists" or artists that may "have a relationship with a particular theater" or if she feels she is "treading in new territory" and needs information. She ended saying "there is definitely material that needs the collaboration between not-for-profits and commercial producers."

David Dower reflected that he was not hearing concerns about the two nonprofit-originated scenarios—either the nonprofit producing a work that is then picked up by a commercial producer, or a nonprofit approaching a commercial producer to assist with undertaking an ambitious work. He asked the nonprofits in the room whether it was work originating in the commercial sector—and specifically the work that comes with the framing, "This is my idea and I need you to do *this*"—that was the most uncomfortable for them.

Brustein replied, "I have no problem either with getting a project suggested to me by commercial producers as long as the commercial producer says, 'It's yours; and when you're finished with it, it's mine again.'" Dower clarified with Brustein that the implication was also that the nonprofit would do its production on its own dime and then would transfer the project to the commercial producer, who would similarly capitalize the Broadway production on its own. Brustein agreed.

Rocco Landesman suggested, however, that Bob Brustein was an outlier on the topic—characterizing him as "Robespierre." Landesman said he suspected almost everyone in the room would agree there is a certain kind of work originating with commercial producers that could happen only through collaboration and that it could be valuable for nonprofit and commercial producers to pursue such work together. Eustis piped up to reiterate that he had never done that and Landesman countered, "But it's the common experience of many people in the room here."

Commercial Producers Carrying On: Pressing On the Issue of Artistic Control

Towards the very end of the day, Oskar Eustis hearkened back to the session on contracts with Michael David and his descriptions of the hands-off approach of Dodger Theatricals and (turning to other commercial producers in the room) said, "That doesn't sound like what you guys have done or feel about it at all. Am I right about that?"

Kevin McCollum said that he would not want any nonprofit to violate its mission by working with him and that from his perspective it all comes down to the pre-production discussions. Landesman then also clarified (as he had the day prior) that Dodger Theatricals was not always hands-off. He shared that when Dodgers produced *Into the Woods* with the Old Globe "most of the elements were already set." He described it as "a pre-Broadway run."

Bob Brustein commented, "So you bossed the whole thing. You rented a theater." Margo Lion weighed in saying that the deals are "not always like that" and Landesman replied, "But they're sometimes like that." Brustein then turned to his former student and current friend, Rocco Landesman, and said he wanted to ask a question about *Big River*. He reiterated that he never understood the production was a "deal" even though Landesman had suggested the director and the composer. Brustein then asked his question and the conversation took a few interesting turns.

> B. Brustein: OK. While I was presumably leading this theater were you giving notes to the director and ... were you carrying on like a Broadway producer?
>
> K. McCollum: We do carry on, don't we? All we do is carry on!
>
> *[laughter]*
>
> R. Landesman: ... Giving notes to the director? I was certainly having conversations with him. Michael David did as well. We were all part of the same group.
>
> K. McCollum: You were making something together.
>
> L. Plotkin: If Bob had wanted to fire the director could he have fired the director? If he thought he wasn't doing a good job?
>
> B. Brustein: Of course, I could have ...
>
> *[Plotkin puts his hand up to Brustein as if to say, "Wait, Let Rocco respond."]*

R. Landesman: If he had wanted to fire him off that production he could have.

S. Frost: Well, it was his contract I would assume—

R. Landesman: I would have objected strenuously …

S. Frost: Sure, but—

R. Landesman: … Bob had the contracts with the director, with the actors, with all of them.

M. Hunt: Objected strenuously, and then what?

B. Brustein: Pardon me?

[Hunt repeats her question while Frost says over her …]

S. Frost: Objected strenuously and let Bob call it because it's his contract.

B. Brustein: That's all he could have done. He could have only objected strenuously. It would have tested our friendship …

R. Landesman: And then what I would have done is, when we took it on, I would have put the director back. And then our friendship was intact.

K. McCollum: Tom Sawyer got everyone to paint his fence.

S. Frost: Can I say, I find it hard to believe that it would be easy for a commercial producer to say, "Here's my show I'll be back opening night." I think it would be very difficult, practically speaking.

B. Brustein: I didn't know it was his show.

S. Frost: No, no, no. But he's speaking of a long history. ... But it doesn't mean that that relationship isn't a positive one. When we did *Memphis* at La Jolla we were there the entire time—the entire time.

O. Eustis: And the director was the artistic director.

S. Frost: Correct.

O. Eustis: That makes a difference.

S. Frost: That made it a lot simpler.

O. Eustis: Just like Des [McAnuff] was [on *Big River*].

K. McCollum: Isn't that worse?

...

T. Taccone: Better for the theater.

K. McCollum: Better for the *artistic director*.

T. Taccone: Better for the *theater*.

S. Frost: It's better for the theater.

Unknown: How is it better for the theater?

T. Taccone: I'm not talking about the product. I'm saying it's better for the theater when a staff member is the central artist, creator.

S. Frost: Absolutely. Totally. But it made it a partnership. It didn't make it an "us" and "them." ... And I rarely *carried on*. ... But what fun is it to not be part of it? You know?

R. Landesman: I was there at the time …

B. Brustein: I know you were part of our company. You had joined our company.

R. Landesman: I wasn't part of the company but I was there.

B. Brustein: You were a collaborator and an adviser—

D. Dower: Let's come back from our breakout groups.

D. Binder: We were both surprised [*pointing to Sue Frost*].

D. Dower: Yes?

S. Frost: By what Michael said. He said, you know, we set it up—blah blah blah blah—and then we come opening night. And we were both like, "Really? I couldn't do that."

D. Binder: Yeah.

S. Frost: I couldn't do that …

O. Eustis: Well, it sounds to me like they don't do that either. Michael just said that they did that.

[*Lots of laugher.*]

The conversation then turned to *Rent* and Jim Nicola explained that he talked to the commercial producers occasionally but he hired the director, the designers, and did all the casting. The commercial producers came to previews and step rehearsals and shared thoughts with Nicola. Oskar Eustis confirmed, again, that this was not a project that had been brought to Nicola by a commercial producer and said, "it just seems to me that it's a very different relationship when Margo has an idea, owns the rights to a property, and starts looking for a nonprofit theater because then ... she's driving the whole bus." Margo Lion responded:

> M. Lion: Oskar, not every relationship is perfect or even works out; but enough of them can work out. I mean, I think it really depends on those meetings of the mind you have with the producer. I mean, the problem is we're tilling the same field. You know, we're both trying to be creative producers, right? Now, that's your mandate, that's your mission. For me, it's not necessarily my mission but that's why I'm in the profession.
>
> O. Eustis: You like to do it.
>
> M. Lion: ... And that's where the problem arises and that's why you've got to agree before you go into it. You've got to have respect and trust. ... That's what makes the relationship work ... And enough of the times, hopefully, you'll have it. And some of the times, you won't. And that's the way it turns out.

Jim Nicola then commented that he didn't see much difference "between a *foundation* saying 'I'll give you this money, for this writer, under these terms,'" or "'I'll give you money for this project, with these terms'" versus a *commercial producer* giving money under certain terms.

Oskar Eustis disagreed, and Nicola continued saying, "Day in and day out, it's making what feels like the best I can of it, to get the resources together. So, if more collaborators are in a room on the producorial side—it's not my favorite way to do it, but occasionally I've felt strongly enough about the artists involved to do that."

I then asked Oskar Eustis whether procuring enhancement money for projects that he originated at The Public changed the goal of the project or put increasing pressure on the piece to move? He responded that he had never taken enhancement and then done something differently with the show because of it; however, he noted (as John Breglio had pointed out) that the enhancement phenomenon was historically very new and that it had been changing just in the six years he had been at The Public. He summed up, "You can feel the temperature changing—people giving money for different reasons than they were a few years back."

Jim Nicola returned to *Rent* and reminded everyone that, again, when he and Kevin McCollum made the agreement to produce the show that they "did not think it was going to be for Broadway." He concluded, "I think the problem is that when you take enhancement money inside the imagination of the artist something occurs that they are headed in a certain direction with certain formal demands that are inescapable." He then admitted (saying directly to Kevin McCollum that he didn't think he had ever mentioned this before) that he had made a pitch to the board of NYTW not to take the enhancement money. He said, "We were short $100,000 and I said, 'There are people at this table that could write that check and we wouldn't have to do this relationship.'" He said the board laughed at him and they took the money.

Kevin McCollum noted that some of those board members even invested in the show and then returned the profits to NYTW. Nicola clarified that he was not complaining about his board—"they're wonderful"— simply pointing out that in this one moment he felt he had failed to make them see what it could have been. McCollum reflected on the fact that he and his partner Jeffrey Seller were "newbies"—he was thirty-two and Seller was thirty—and that they just "wanted to do a musical that they would want to go to."

Michael Friedman then spoke up to say:

> You guys made a *thing*. ... You succeeded. ... I got to New York in 1997 and for all of us who got to New York after *Rent* opened on Broadway, it was a changed landscape. Probably only *Hair* and *Chorus Line* changed the landscape as much, in the sense of changing the entire expectation level of everything.... So, in a funny way I would say "enhancement shmenhancement"—it's almost like because of that show if you write a musical and are

at a not-for-profit, if you do not go to the Nederlander and run for seven years, twelve years, fifteen years, you've failed. ... The definition of success—that's transformed for all of us.

The Definition of Success Has Been Transformed: Can We Really Change It Back?

Picking up on Friedman's comments and echoing Jim Nicola, Eustis said, "That's the thing we need even more than an ethics statement—we need an alternative definition of success." He then shared an experience of working with an artist that had a successful run at The Public but who was sincerely disappointed that the work was not moving to Broadway. Eustis asked the room, "How do you make the whole enterprise feel victorious at the highest level without it having to be a commercial hit? I don't think we know how to do that anymore in the nonprofit theater." David Binder agreed.

> D. Binder: Artists feel like if they get their show on and it gets great reviews and it sells out the six weeks at The Public or the, wherever—
>
> O. Eustis: The only question is "What's next?"
>
> D. Binder: What's next? Are we going to Broadway? Are we not going to Broadway? Because now Off-Broadway's not really an option. So it's either a success or it's a failure, based on that. [Sighs and shakes his head.] That's horrible.
>
> O. Eustis: We've got to change that ...

John Breglio then asked Eustis about *Passing Strange*, which was a critical and artistic success but not a commercial success in its Broadway run. Breglio made the point that one of the dangers of a nonprofit going this route is that it can change the definition of success (and change a production from being perceived as a success to being perceived as a failure) if expectations going into the Broadway production are not clearly understood up front. Eustis pointed out that he did not have this problem with his board and that no one at The Public cared if the show made money or not on Broadway—but he was quite aware that he was unable to finish *Passing Strange* without the financial investments of Liz McCann and Gerry Schoenfeld. "I wrestle with the situation where, again, the only way that my show, my artists, can be completely successful is if somebody else does it. That feels—not so good. It feels not correct."

Michael Friedman then challenged the room to think of a noncommercial Off-Broadway musical that had not moved to Broadway in the past eight to ten years that everyone actually thinks of as being a great success. After a long silence Margo Lion said, "You can't do it anymore." A couple of productions were mentioned but it was agreed that these were exceptions that proved the rule.

John Breglio mentioned, again, the impact of the loss of commercial Off-Broadway and Michael Friedman said that he was quite aware of that loss. Margo Lion then asked Oskar Eustis if he felt that *Caroline, or Change* would have gone on to have a successful life if it had not had a run on Broadway. Eustis responded that it's impossible to know with certainty but that he felt it would have and that he believed Tony Kushner felt that the Broadway move had been essential to its moving into the repertory. Friedman also acknowledged that he thought the situation was different for plays—which can have some success in the regions even if they do not have a Broadway run.

David Binder asked, "How can we create success for artists that is not contextualized on whether the show moves to Broadway?" to which Margo Lion responded, "I hate to say it, but it's like wanting to play in the World Series." Gregory Mosher pounced on Lion's analogy.

G. Mosher: No! No! I'm sorry to be rude. Samuel Beckett's goal was not to play on Broadway. Pinter's goal was not to play on. … Brecht's goal was not to play on Broadway! It's a bad analogy. Sorry to jump on you.

M. Lion: No, no. Greg, I agree with you. … And it has to do with the culture, I agree. It's not like I think Broadway is necessarily any home for great artistic ventures. But artists want their work on Broadway because that's the way they can—

G. Mosher: No!

O. Eustis: Greg, Greg, it's not true. American playwrights currently writing do, *they do*.

G. Mosher: *Because*, I would say, we have still not—and I'm not flagellating any of us—but we have not created an alternative by which you can make a living in the not-for-profit theater. So, of course, they want to go to Broadway. That's all they got!

…

M. Lion: No, it's visibility, Greg. It's not just a living, it's *visibility*. They want to be written up. They want to have a chance at awards. They want to, you know, they want to be in the discussion; but they're afraid they're not going to be in the discussion if they aren't produced on Broadway.

D. Binder: See, that's what I'm saying. That was my question.

M. Friedman: I think running for a long time is part of it. But the fact is you cannot run for a long time now. You cannot. … *Hedwig*, actually would be the last one that I know, and I know it's commercial. … But at the time, I think you guys felt really excited about how long you had run at James St.

D. Binder: Yeah. Yes.

M. Friedman: Very successfully. It was a successful run.

M. Lion: Today it would have had to go to Broadway.

IN THE INTERSECTION

> D. Binder: ... I want to ask this question: How do we make artists feel that they have succeeded in their six-week run at The Public?

A couple ideas were tossed out: Was it about making artists eligible for Tony awards? Was it about making the production into an event? But there was a palpable sense that it was very hard for the nonprofit theater to compete with Broadway in terms of legitimating new musicals.

Thus, as the two-day discussion began to wind down, it came full circle to the conversation that began with Rocco Landesman and Gregory Mosher, who had diagnosed the underlying issue as one of shifting measures of success. Success defined in terms of Broadway runs, Tony awards, box office success, stars, and all the other "bells and whistles."

TOWARDS THE CREATION OF A STATEMENT

Moderated by David Dower

> It seems to me more than anything else, what the not-for-profit sector, what the resident theater sector can use more than anything else, is a kind of booster shot of idealism.—Rocco Landesman

A Proposal: The Creation of a Statement to Guide Collaborations in the Intersection

As mentioned earlier, at one point in the full group discussion David Dower said he wanted to try to take advantage of one of the destinations to which the conversation seemed to be heading: towards the creation of a statement that could serve as a guide post for collaborations in the intersection between the nonprofit and commercial theater sectors. Dower was not proposing that the group draft the statement, per se, but rather discuss the kinds of areas that such a statement might cover. He then called on Rocco Landesman to share thoughts that he had discussed with Dower during a break.

Landesman commented on the fact that one of the subjects of the meeting was the initial impulse of the resident theater movement (how it was set up and why it was done) and that there was a general consensus that "we've moved some distance away from that." He continued:

> Things have become blurred and muddled and the mission has diffused largely because of exigencies, realities, necessities. But it

seems to me, more than anything else, what the not-for-profit sector, what the resident theater sector, can use more than anything else, is a kind of booster shot of idealism—of a kind of return to what we were starting out to do and what we might do to get there or to get back to that a little bit. Jim raised the issue before about could we put together just a page or two, a kind of statement about what we're about, what we want to do, and maybe some parameters about how we view what we would ideally like to do. I don't think it needs to be programmatic; but what we'd ideally like our relationship with the for-profit sector [to be] … and how we envision ourselves (ourselves being the not-for-profit sector) as we go forward. Now, I think probably some consensus could come around that towards a statement of ideals and principles that wouldn't have to bind anybody. It's not going to be programmatic and specific. But I don't think it's a bad idea to reset what we're about and what our ideals and hopes are for our world going forward.

Several concerns, questions, and suggestions were raised with regard to the proposed exercise:

- Landesman himself acknowledged that theaters not present might not be eager to sign on to a statement; however, he didn't see this as a reason not to move forward.

- Kevin Moore noted that the meeting itself consisted of only a small group of white middle-aged individuals. He expressed a concern about this group speaking on behalf of a field of almost 2,000 nonprofit theaters. In response, Gregory Mosher suggested that the group speak for itself and not for the field, and Kevin McCollum suggested that, in addition to whatever paper might emerge from the meeting, a survey could be utilized to capture perspectives across the field.

- Several people raised their hands to get clarification on the goal of the exercise: Should the group be identifying a set of common *practices* or *actions* that might distinguish some nonprofits (a manifesto, of sorts)? Was the statement meant to be a *value proposition*—a statement of the value that nonprofits provide to their communities in exchange for investment—or was the statement meant to be simply a list of *core values* to which nonprofits should commit? Jim Nicola pointed out that what he had been hoping for (among other things perhaps) was a suggestion of the *ethical* relationship between the two sectors.

Dower suggested that in the limited time remaining it was unreasonable to think the group could come to agreement on what the statement should be, much less write a manifesto, but that perhaps every person could simply share a few thoughts on what would make such a statement helpful, or meaningful, from his or her standpoint.

Paper and pencils were distributed and the group took ten minutes to write down their thoughts.

***

The Ideas that Could be Included in a Statement

David Dower asked if there was anyone who felt comfortable starting. He reminded the group that the goal was not to wordsmith a statement; rather, to simply understand the values and ideas present in the circle and then to discuss them a little bit. The ideas generally seemed to be of four types: those seeking to require organizations to do more for artists; those seeking to require organizations to do more for their communities; those seeking to require nonprofits to clarify their purpose or mission; and those seeking to restrict nonprofits from engaging in activities that would compromise their missions. What follows are the statements shared by the group and brief discussions about them.

Bob Brustein opened with:

1. "One, no enhancement. Two, no prior partnerships. Three, compensation (or royalties) only after the show has been

produced and the theater is approached by a commercial theater."

Rocco Landesman replied, "That's going to be a nonstarter for 90 percent of theaters," but Dower encouraged more ideas to be put on the table.

Gregory Mosher suggested that his was the "anti-seduce-the-artistic-director or managing director" statement:

2. "My theater X will embark on no partnership or collaboration with any commercial producer without a thorough and even exhaustive discussion with the staff, key artists, and boards of my theater, and we will undergo that process on each and every project, to discuss the pros and cons of such a partnership or collaboration."

Landesman had two statements:

3. "Resident theaters must redouble their vigilance in preserving their artistic autonomy and authority in their ventures with commercial producers ... and those ventures shouldn't even be initiated if the work is in any way at variance with the artistic mission and normal operations of the theater."

4. "Resident theaters must scale up their support of artists, whether that means increasing compensation or permanent employment and health care or other forms of security and validation."

Oskar Eustis read what he wrote, clarifying that the "us" referred to nonprofit institutions:

5. "We are here to support art that the marketplace cannot support and we are here to reach audiences other than on their ability to pay. On the basis of those principles, no theater deserves philanthropic support that doesn't have artists on its fulltime staff

and theaters should not take subsidiary rights from playwrights. Artists shouldn't be subsidizing the institutions."

He commented in jest that he promised to make really good use of money from commercial producers if they gave it to him, but then made the serious comment that "clarity about those relationships" seemed very important to him. He remarked that he was "all over this question of nonprofit theaters getting clear and better about what they're doing."

Tony Taccone jumped in to say his declaration was very similar and that the title of his statement was, "What is the not-for-profit theater?" He suggested:

6. The document should open with a brief statement as to the values that inspired the field to invent itself and what the group perceived to be the problem that necessitates the conversation back and forth.

Taccone then said that his statement would include the following:

7. Re-education of the board in terms of mission, a safe home for artists, primacy for artists, the reassertion of the identity of a town in America (a community), and the primacy of originality.

Dower asked Taccone if he had identified the "problem" and Taccone replied that he had not but did not think it would be hard to do so.

Bob Brustein interjected for a moment to ask whether people noticed that the name had changed from nonprofit to not-for-profit and the significance of this: the former says, essentially, theaters won't make a profit and the second implies theaters are not primarily interested in profits but can make them. Kevin McCollum countered that when he ran a nonprofit that profits were called surpluses and were ploughed back into the theater.

McCollum began by suggesting:

8. **The mission for a theater can be anything as long as it both fulfills the obligations of the IRS and serves the community, where the theater is based (that is, is relevant to that community).**

He then opined that "capitalism at its best might be the idea of collaboration" and offered:

9. **Commercial and nonprofit producers might work together to bring people into a dark space and make sure they leave somehow transformed and inspired.**

And then offered:

10. **Every not-for-profit should work in their local town to make sure that every eighth grader is in a musical and to make sure that the arts aren't taken out of school, because we've shifted from an arts model (coming together to articulate a better story) to a sports model (dividing into teams and competing).**

McCollum pleaded with the nonprofits in the room not to be divisive and to trust the commercial producers, whom he characterized as "lacking communities" but having ideas, having relationships that everyone could benefit from, and wanting to tell stories. Mosher quickly interjected to say that he was not suggesting that nonprofits should not talk to commercial producers, only that nonprofits should not take an action blindly.

I put forward the following suggestion:

11. **Transparency in all 990 filings, financials, and grant applications about enhancement money, royalties, and artistic control.**

Sue Frost said that she had been thinking about where the interests of nonprofit and commercial producers align and where they differ and what "each brings to the table to make the whole stronger." She offered:

12. The commercial and nonprofit theater have common priorities: artist support, long- term development of new work, and audiences for that work. The two sectors need to work toward transparency around expectations, examining definitions of "success," strengthening tolerance for risk, and more clearly defining the research and development, manufacturing, and distribution processes at the intersection.

Kevin Moore said that he would like to see the following:

13. More time and energy spent recruiting board members that "love your theater" rather than those that "have the biggest checkbooks."

14. Nonprofit theaters called something else—mission driven theaters or some other term that does not invoke money.

Taccone asked why and Moore replied that the conversation had come to be one about money. Mara Isaacs offered that "a lot of times it is about money." Moore agreed but said he was not sure that money should be the first thing taken into consideration. I shared with Moore that Claire Gaudiani had written a piece a few years back suggesting the term "social profit" instead of nonprofit. Moore continued, saying:

15. There needs to be more buy-in to the mission throughout organizations and nonprofit theaters need to recommit, as part of their missions, to changing the world.

John Breglio spoke up next. He first commented that while the statements proposed by Bob Brustein might be appropriate for a particular not-for-profit (suggesting as an example The Public Theater under Joseph Papp), they would not be appropriate for *all* theaters. He made the point that different theaters need different identities saying, "The shoe that fits the little company in Milwaukee is never going to fit the

Roundabout; but they're both worthy not-for-profits." Breglio then read his statement:

16. "This theater's imperative and purpose, for all of its productions, whether produced solely with its own resources, or in collaboration with any third parties, will be to produce theatrical works of artistic merit, for all audiences, in accordance with its not-for-profit mission."

Eustis responded, asking whether Breglio could imagine a single theater in the country that would disagree with the statement. Smith seconded Eustis's point and added that most of the theaters sitting around the circle had strong artistic missions already. Breglio replied that he was simply suggesting that if not-for-profits were being consistent with their not-for-profit missions that they would not run into trouble in the intersection. He suggested that the statement, at a minimum, might suggest that "you can work alone or with others as long as you are producing consistent with your purpose and producing plays of artistic merit—unless you disagree with working with people outside."

Bob Brustein picked up on Breglio's last point and said that he did, indeed, disagree with working with people outside as doing so was the "beginning of the corruption of the theater." He asserted a theater must follow its own vision. He also expressed concerns regarding Breglio's "eloquent statement," saying it was subject to a lot of interpretation and that a theater could ostensibly agree with the statement but in practice be doing something diametrically opposed to it. He then reasserted the need for:

17. Clear, very simple statements outlining what nonprofit theaters are and how they do and don't behave.

Margo Lion jumped in to say that she loved Bob Brustein, but disagreed with him on this front. She said that she agreed with John Breglio, and that if a nonprofit theater actually followed such tenets that it would be doing what it needed to do. She then added the items from her list:

18. "A home for artists."

19. An imperative to grow the audience demographic "because this country is changing and we will not have anyone going to the theater if we don't make that a top concern."

Eustis then suggested that the group:

21. Replace the term "home for artists" with "salaried staff position with benefits for artists" because every theater in America says it provides a home for artists. "If we were to say something that's wrong with the not-for-profit theater—one of the things—institutions have grown in a way that they've become self-perpetuating institutions rather than places that support artists."

He clarified that the artist position should not be an administrative post (like that of an artistic director) and suggested that one artist on salary with benefits should be the minimum criteria. He continued: "Most of the theaters in this country, including the ones with eight-figure budgets, have no artists on salary. They don't pay benefits or healthcare for artists. They don't and they should. Start with one, but there should be a lot more than that."

Molly Smith then prefaced her recommendations for the statement by stating her vision for nonprofits and commercial theaters in the intersection: "The relationship between the theater and the commercial producer drives through the heart of the mission of the theater and includes a relationship to the community." She then suggested that the statement needed to include:

22. Something about the mutual building of community—meaning commercial producers should not simply fly in and fly out without taking an interest in the community.

Smith said that community was, from her perspective, the big piece that was missing. A bit later Taccone pressed a bit on Molly Smith's statements about community and asked what that sounded like to commercial producers in the room. Kevin McCollum said that this had very much been his experience—getting to know the local community and making himself available for dinners and meetings with board members, for example. Smith followed up saying that what she meant by the statement was also, on a very practical level:

23. Understanding who is in the audience and perhaps developing shared goals around building an audience for a particular kind of work.

McCollum, picking up on Smith's comments, then asked whether there was something to be learned from the blockbuster exhibitions model used by museums. McCollum said he was intrigued by the fact that museums regularly pull together high profile exhibitions in partnership with others and wondered how they get such exhibitions funded and whether there would be language or practices in the museum world that could be applicable to the intersection.

Several people spoke up to suggest that the museum model was quite different than the theater model. Mame Hunt suggested that the museums are different because they begin planning many years in advance, and that the content in museums, dance, and music was not "threatening" in the same way that content in theater could be. Mara Isaacs suggested that the difference was in audience: theater requires a group of people to come together at a particular moment in time to experience an event. However, McCollum responded that he also plans years in advance and that "Mapplethorpe killed arts funding" and was considered quite threatening, and that waiting in line to see a great exhibit could be a type of theatrical event. Eustis pointed out that generally no one whose work is exhibited is paid by the museum—works are generally borrowed. Eustis then asked for my thoughts on the subject. I shared that it was difficult to generalize and that, in many ways, the art world had similar struggles to the theater—that there had been concerns expressed and questions raised in recent years about inappropriate relationships between, or practices by, the various actors in the art world (i.e., dealers, collectors, museums, auction houses, and commercial galleries).

Mara Isaacs then shared her thoughts on the statement, saying:

24. Institutions need to reinvest in, refine, and articulate their institutional purpose and vision with an understanding of their personal definition of success; to resist the inexorable pull of market forces; and to reestablish themselves as community leaders, as places that sustain artists, and as places to express a core set of values.

She then shared the question that she asks herself whenever considering a partnership or other significant programming decision:

25. "What is the need? What are the options available to fill that need? Have you truly thought through all of your options? Are you being honest with yourself? Are you using your intuition? And are you choices reflecting your central purpose or mission?"

There was a tremendously positive response to the list of questions with many people murmuring such things as "very good" and "good questions."

Jim Nicola then said he felt confused by some of the more specific proscriptions and prescriptions: "no enhancement" and "artists on salary." He suggested that if everyone agreed on "no enhancement," it would happen anyway and that it would just be a matter of time before lawyers came up with a new name for it and a way of making it happen. He also said that while he agreed in principle with the idea of more support for artists that it was very difficult for him to envision putting artists on salary given his mission and structure as an organization. He made the following suggestion:

26. The statement move away from specific practices towards "ideas, values, and ethics." It should include "a very clearly articulated measure of success that excludes commercial transfer."

Nicola added that commercial transfer *could* be a measure of success, "but what are the other ones?"

David Binder's suggestion was:

27. Nonprofit "organizations should lead their buildings": meaning, buildings should serve organizations rather than organizations serve buildings.

Dower asked Binder how this would benefit him as a commercial producer and Binder said he wasn't thinking about how it would benefit commercial producers but felt it was, nonetheless, important. He elaborated saying that the commercial producers were in the room because they perceive that "we're all in this together." They believe that if the nonprofit theater is strong it will benefit everyone. He ended, "In the theater we all fail or we all succeed has always been my point of view."

Polly Carl then spoke up and said she had been thinking of the hyperbole that comes with mission statements and then shared her thoughts for what was needed instead:

28. "What nonprofits really need are ethics statements" (something she had never seen from a nonprofit) that would include such things as concrete support for artists, the ratio between the highest and lowest salaried position, and the ratio of earned to unearned income. There has to be "some sort of truth" to such ethics statements and the goal should be transparency.

Carl ended saying, "Wall Street is Wall Street because they don't have an ethics statement."

Dower then reflected that he had been listening to the conversation with an ear to hearing whether there was "a community interest." Dower wondered whether what's needed in the world at the moment is for the nonprofit and commercial theater to define the intersection as a shared responsibility rather than it simply being "on the nonprofits" to get its house in order.

Nicola responded that he thought an ethics statement was "a genius idea" and that he would want to include not only statements concerning the operations of a nonprofit but, specifically, its relationship (if it were to have one) with the commercial theater. Brustein then suggested that there was both a practical and ethical reason for having an association with a training program. The practical reasons have to do with developing new talent but the ethical reason is that "young people are the ones that keep us honest."

Dower called on Loren Plotkin to see if he had written anything down for the statement. Plotkin reflected that the thing he had been most struck by in his conversation with nonprofits was the "definition of success and how that had affected them profoundly." He said:

29. The definition of success in nonprofits needs to be examined in a very serious way.

He added soberly, "I'm not sure you can do anything about it; our society has changed."

Dower suggested that perhaps a clear statement of ethics could help in this regard and McCollum tagged on that such a statement should also include a clear statement regarding the relationship with the press. McCollum repeated a phrase someone had used earlier, "We'll play by any rules the press wants to play by—but what are the rules?"

Edgar Dobie then shared his thoughts on the statement, picking up on Bob Brustein's rule, "Don't take any enhancement money" and he added a modification and condition:

30. "Only accept enhancement—and it should be rigorously examined as you suggest—if you have the right to continue the project if the commercial producer wants to abandon the idea or disagrees with you."

Dobie asserted that such a condition would be an attempt to address the issue of control; however, he acknowledged that it would mean the nonprofit would also need to have the resources to follow through—meaning it would need to exercise caution and discipline. He added that there was one more thing he would write into his manifesto:

31. "Don't let anyone get between you and the relationship with the writer."

ACKNOWLEDGMENTS

I feel privileged to have been invited by David Dower and Polly Carl to participate in this meeting and to write the public report of the proceedings. Thanks are due to many. First and foremost, I am grateful to the participants themselves, for responding favorably to the invitation to meet and discuss partnerships between commercial and nonprofit theaters; for talking with each other openly and with respect, humor, and courage; and for carefully reviewing the report and giving approval for their comments to be shared publicly. Next, I would be remiss if I did not give special thanks to Emerson College and the Center for the Theater Commons for supporting the creation, publication, and dissemination of this report. I am also grateful to Vijay Mathew and Jamie Gahlon, for managing many aspects of the meeting and publication; to Pablo Halpern for preparation of the background readings; and to Caroline Baron, Kevin Becerra, Erin Daley, Allycia Jones, Rachel Knox, Marissa La Rose, Aaron Malkin, Daniel Pruksarnukul, Laura Raines, Amrita Ramanan, and Erin Washington for note taking and video recording of the meeting. Finally, I am indebted to Polly Carl and Lynette D'Amico for direction, comments, and edits on the report and to David Dower for his leadership and excellent moderation of the discussion. My job was made easier because they performed theirs so well. It is a gift to do work one loves and to do so alongside those one counts as friends. This project allowed me to do so and for that I am particularly thankful.

PARTICIPANTS

(listed within the categories that most
accurately convey their *current* roles)

Nonprofit Theater Representatives:[18]

Christopher Ashley	Artistic Director, La Jolla Playhouse
Polly Carl	Director, Center for the Theater Commons, Emerson College Editor, HowlRound
Edgar Dobie	Managing Director, Arena Stage
David Dower	Director of Artistic Programs, ArtsEmerson, Emerson College
Oskar Eustis	Artistic Director, The Public Theatre
Mame Hunt	Dramaturg, Sundance Theatre Institute
Mara Isaacs	Producing Director, McCarter Theatre Center
James Nicola	Artistic Director, New York Theatre Workshop
Molly Smith	Artistic Director, Arena Stage
Tony Taccone	Artistic Director, Berkeley Repertory Theatre

---

[18]Both Michael Ritchie, Artistic Director of Center Theatre Group, and Zelda Fichandler, Founding Artistic Director of Arena Stage, planned to attend the In the Intersection meeting but were ultimately unable to do so due to unforeseen circumstances. Also, at the time of the meeting Polly Carl and David Dower worked at Arena Stage.

IN THE INTERSECTION

Commercial Producers:

David Binder	David Binder Productions
John F. Breglio	Producer (and former entertainment attorney)

Commercial Producers:

Michael David	Producer, Dodger Theatricals
Sue Frost	Producer, Junk Yard Dog Productions
Margo Lion	Producer, Margo Lion Ltd.
Gregory Mosher	Producer/Director
Kevin McCollum	Alchemation

Artists:

Robert Brustein	Playwright, Critic, Producer, Educator & Founding Director, American Repertory Theater
Michael Friedman	Composer
Amy Freed	Playwright
Charles Randolph-Wright	Playwright
Karen Zacarias	Playwright

Other:

Rocco Landesman	Chairman, National Endowment of the Arts
Kevin Moore	Managing Director, Theatre Communications Group
Loren Plotkin	Attorney
Diane Ragsdale	Doctoral Student & Lecturer, Erasmus University, Meeting Documentarian

www.ingramcontent.com/pod-product-compliance
Lightning Source LLC
Chambersburg PA
CBHW071215090426
42736CB00014B/2837